Making
Victorian Dolls' House
Furniture

Making
Victorian Dolls' House
Furniture

Patricia King

GUILD OF MASTER CRAFTSMAN PUBLICATIONS LTD

First published 1995 by
Guild of Master Craftsman Publications Ltd
166 High Street, Lewes
East Sussex BN7 1XU

ISBN 0 946819 56 4

Photography © Steve Hawkins
Line illustrations © Rod King

Designed by Teresa Dearlove

Typefaces: Futura and Belwe

Origination in Singapore under the supervision of MRM Graphics.
Printed in Hong Kong by H & Y Printing Co.

Foreword

Once in a great while, someone who is unique enters my life. One such person is Patricia King. To know this lady is to love her. She has a vitality and spirit that encompasses everything she does.

There is a phenomenal interest in dolls' houses and rooms which has grown through the years. Today the land of Lilliput is made up of many different ideas and attitudes and Pat brings her own individual contribution to miniatura. She makes use of the mundane and of bric-a-brac in ways that astound. She sees the possibilities in objects that ordinarily would end up in the trash basket. Her creative juices flow with boundless imagination. Miniaturists everywhere benefit from her remarkable and surprising rendition of Victorian furnishings and accessories.

Pat is a natural teacher. A ceramicist by profession, she exudes enthusiasm to her students and translates this same vitality to her writing.

She obviously likes people and being among them, which sets her above the ordinary. Everyone benefits from such associations. Devoted to her wonderful family, she takes time to be with them, indulging them in creative and exciting ways. How fortunate for them.

Yes, Pat is unique and I cherish her as a friend.

Helen K. Ruthberg

Contents

To Drew, our special treasure, and to the memory of Jamie

Acknowledgements

My thanks to my editor Lindy Dunlop who worked with me and cheerfully gave her expertise and experience to make the scraps I gave her into a coat of many colours.

Introduction

Anyone who has looked at an odd earring and thought, 'It's a shame to throw that away, it might come in useful,' is my sort of person! I lack the skills to do much work using tools, so when I started modelling I looked for things that could be used as they were or with just a little adaptation. With some imagination and improvisation, beautiful things can be made with little expense. Making dolls' house furniture from throwaway odds and ends is fascinating and recycling is in, with collection bins in every town for newspapers, bottles and the like.

Many people stow away little treasures and often as not, they will happily give them to you if you can make something nice from them. I like to think that I can put anything small to use and knowing this, friends often give me odds and ends. I see it as a challenge to make something impressive from these.

Sometimes an item will inspire me and the idea for a room or piece of furniture will develop around it. At other times, I have the idea of what I want firmly in my mind and have to go in search of materials to make it. This was the case with the conservatory, seen later in the book, but I did eventually find the wherewithal and I am very pleased with the result.

Dolls' house modelling fascinates me and I have started to view the world in terms of making miniatures: staying in a hotel or drinking in a pub, if I see something I like (a clock, a cupboard, a chair), my mind translates it into materials I could use to model it. Right there a wireless face can become a ring pull and its knobs bead caps. There is endless inspiration.

Collecting is no less an interest. I now have boxes of odds and ends but am always on the lookout for more. It gets to the stage where you choose your cafe for the things you can take away rather than for the food. Single portion butter and jam containers come in many shapes and sizes and make wonderful sinks. You can even make a corner sink from some of these. The plastic tubs you get paté in make excellent baths, and tea stirrers can be used for many things.

This book is about ideas. In each project I have told you what I used, but you can adapt these to suit yourself. The pieces you make will differ from mine because your materials won't be the same. It is often the way, with this sort of modelling, that an original idea will be modified or changed by the pieces that you have or that you find along the way and this is half the fun! You never know quite what to expect. Experimentation is the key, but here, at least, are some ideas to put your saved treasures to good use.

Safety

While there are no power tools or highly volatile liquids used in making any of the projects in this book, the question of safety still needs to be considered. Accidents by their nature are unexpected, but they can be avoided by following basic common sense and safety rules.

☛ Keep your workspace clean. Wipe up spills when they happen and keep the floor clear. It is easy to knock something from a crowded bench onto your foot, or to slip, or trip and fall.

☛ Keep a first-aid kit close by, in a visible and easily accessible place. Nothing elaborate is needed, but make sure that it is kept well stocked.

☛ Many paints are solvent based so store and use them in a well-ventilated place. Keep paint containers closed when they are not in use. When spray painting, spray outside if possible, avoid inhaling fumes, and keep your eyes protected.

☛ Keep all tools and materials out of reach of children.

☛ Glue guns use heated glue. When pressing together pieces bound with such hot glue, use a pencil to apply pressure: if you use your fingers you may lose your fingerprints.

1 Tools and Techniques

The best methods for this craft are those which you develop as you work, so the points below are suggestions rather than instructions – adopt, adapt or ignore them as you please!

Tools

I don't use many tools and try to avoid them if possible, but there are some that I use a lot and they are very handy to have. The few that I do recommend are: **ruler, scissors,** files, leather punch, pliers, modeller's scalpel, wire cutters, modeller's saw, glass cutter.

Glue gun

A glue gun is very useful with this kind of work where individual elements are not made to fit each other. Joining two things of differing shape can be difficult, but using a glue gun, you can easily form a pad of glue to act as a joint or buffer between the two surfaces.

Gluing

I have found two types of glue that I am happy with. These are Copydex and the glue gun which uses a solid glue stick. Both can be bought from hardware stores and craft shops.

Copydex is a rubber based glue that doesn't penetrate materials so it is excellent for upholstering and making dolls – for anything that involves gluing fabrics and trimmings.

My glue gun is a marvellous discovery and I use it all the time. All you need do is put the glue stick into the gun, plug it in and you're all set to create! It is fast, gives you time to adjust pieces that are not quite right before the glue sets, and you can form pads of glue to act as joints, binding objects and surfaces of different shapes.

Spray painting

Spray painting is the best and the fastest way I have found for uniting the disparate pieces of my furniture and giving them an acceptable finish. The paint I use is the cellulose paint used for automobile repairs. Good ventilation is vital when using this paint so it is best to spray only in the open air. The fine spray produced gets into the smallest details without clogging and obscuring them, the paint dries very quickly and gives a waterproof coating.

Cellulose paints are available in DIY stores and come in a wide range of colour and finish. I prefer the metallic finish paints because I like the sparkle they give. Metallic finish paints have 'met' written on the can.

Remember to spray your pieces from all angles. I use a potter's wheel to spin them though a cake decorating stand would do just as well and there is nothing to stop you turning them by hand. When the first coat has dried, turn the piece upside down and spray it from underneath.

It is fun to mix paints to get different effects. For an antique look, you can get an old, speckled effect by dusting one colour over another.

I suggest you cover your clothes when spraying, but if you get paint on your hands, it comes off easily with nail polish remover.

For touching up a missed bit or giving individual parts special treatment, I use watercolours. By first running your brush over a bar of soap, you will be able to paint on a shiny surface. Only a little soap is needed – if it froths there is too much.

2 Finding Materials

Because you are not looking for specific things but for shapes and textures that remind you of objects or that inspire you to make something from them, you can find things in the most unexpected places. There are some things that I find I use a lot so I have listed these, and where to find them, below. Most importantly, don't limit yourself — almost anything can be used!

Jumble sales and bric-a-brac stores

Beads, single or stranded
Bead caps (you will often find these
    between the beads of a necklace)
Bracelets and bracelet links
Bangles
Buckles
Belts
Belt-hole eyelets
Necklace clasps
Cuff links
Charms
Brooches
Watch parts
Chesspieces
Buttons
Home perm curlers
Toy fencing and railing
Little bells

Consumer goods/packaging

Bubble packs
Cigar tubes
Lipstick cylinders
Toilet cylinders
Biro casing
Pill capsules and bottles
Toothpaste lids
Paint and ointment tubes
Felt pen lids
Cartridges

Takeaway foods and cafés

Single serve butter, jam and milk
    containers
Miniature drink bottles
Pizza lid supporters
Drinking straws
Ring pulls
Toothpicks
Cocktail sticks
Tea stirrers

There are other things that are not so easy
to find second-hand. If you can't find
them, here is where they can be bought.

Newsagents and stationers

Map pins
Pins
Acco fasteners
Paper clips
Card
Giftwrap
Paper
Fablon
Sellotape
Pipe cleaners

Florists

Green tape
Oasis
Frogs
Gutta percha

Haberdashers

Fabric
Trimmings
Lampshade gimp

Hardware stores

Olives
Drawer handles
Polyfilla

Supermarkets and health food stores

Wedding cake columns
Wedding cake bells
Embossed cake foil
Christmas tree light holders

Angler's shops

Hooks
Flies
Feathers

Toy shops

Miniature
    fencing and
    railing
Fimo

DIY stores

Plywood (6mm for bases, 4mm for walls)
Copydex
Stick-on moulding
Balsa

Art supply shops

Foamcore
Dry-print lettering
Card

Finally, there are many hobby and
modellers' outlets catering for dolls'
house and modellers' needs, and dolls'
house furnishings and accessories are
available commercially.

3 Tips and Hints

ollecting materials is an important part of the modelling process, the next step being transformation. Here are some ideas for putting collected materials to use, though as you work you will find your own uses.

Using materials

The fussiness of filigree buckles and bracelets, fancy bead caps and buttons help to give a Victorian look to pieces. You

can flatten a bead cap to give an intricate design or use it for a handle surround. A bangle around the side of a table top will give an antique feel as will small links used for maker's nameplates.

It can be hard to find matching pieces to make a set of chairs. Drawer handles, however, can be bought in a set and if you are lucky enough to find a link bracelet or belt, these will give you matching backs. Both drawer handles and florist's frogs can be used for stools as they are.

Table legs can be plain or decorative. Choose your materials to suit what you want. For the central leg of a small table, chesspieces are very good. Cut off their heads and you will be left with a carved leg and a flat surface to support the table top. You can also set the chesspiece on a button or brooch to give it a base. Home perm curlers also make good

legs and an advantage in using these is that it is quite easy to get a matching set. For feet, glue beads to the bottom corners of your piece.

Toothpaste lids topped with buttons, shaft up, will give you canisters and can also be used to form part of a fancy table leg. A bead cap with the eye from a hook and eye fastener makes a decorative drawer handle and surround. Bead caps can also be used to hold and secure round objects. A bangle opened up becomes a fireguard. Cuts of Biro can be used for lamps, tumblers and glasses.

If you don't have a brooch use a button, if you have no wire, an invisible hair pin will do. If there is anything that you can't find, adapt something else and use it.

Pile-ups

Often in my instructions I refer to a 'pile-up' job. In these, the project is made by assembling all its constituent pieces, one on top of the other. The job is made easier if you first make a central hole in each piece, where possible, and thread a wire through them as you assemble. The extra stability this gives makes for easier handling prior to gluing.

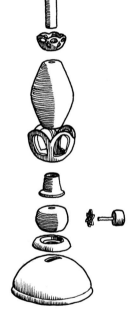

Scale

If you have trouble determining the scale of your pieces, make a simple pipe cleaner doll, about 5in (12.5cm) tall, and use this to judge size. Seat or stand the doll at your pieces and compare where your dolls' house furniture comes up to them with where your life-size furniture comes up to you.

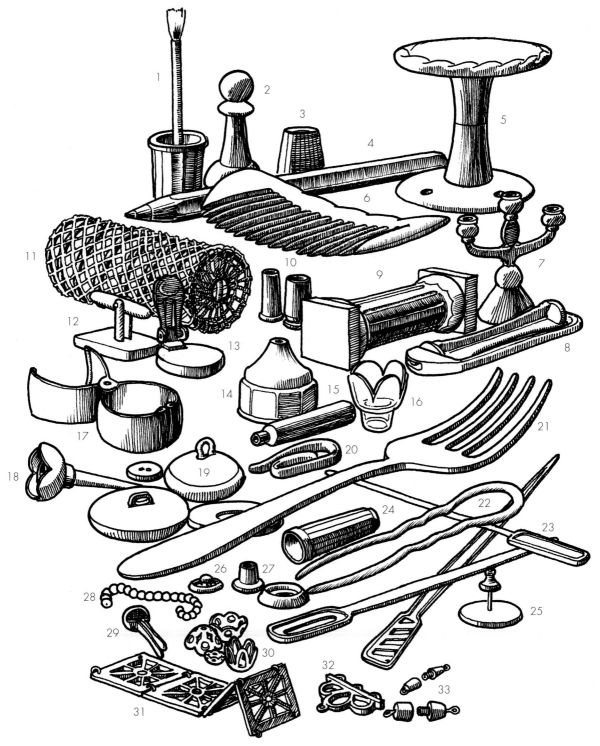

1 Tippex bottle top	10 Brass cartridge cases	19 Buttons	28 Ball-and-socket bobble
2 Chesspiece	11 Net-covered spring hair curler	20 Curtain hook	chain
3 Toothpaste tube cap	12 Cuff link	21 Fork	29 Paper fastener
4 Biro	13 Clip-on earring	22 Chignon pin	30 Bead caps
5 Drawer handle	14 Saltcellar pourer top	23 Plastic tea stirrers	31 Decorative link bracelet
6 Fancy hair comb	15 Ink cartridge	24 Felt-tip pen lid	32 Three-into-one necklace
7 Miniature brass candle holder	16 Christmas tree light holder	25 Earring bell	fastener
8 Home perm curler	17 Glove clip	26 Press stud fastener	33 Screw-type necklace
9 Wedding cake column	18 Birthday cake candle holder	27 Metal eyelet	fasteners

4 Basic Boxes

Boxes form the basis of most of my models, from the individual pieces to the rooms they are displayed in, to the dolls' house itself, which is really a collection of boxes. Sometimes you will be lucky enough to find a ready-made box that you can build on: 35mm film boxes and matchboxes can be very handy. More often this is not the case and you will need to make a box to suit your particular needs.

Furniture

For furniture I make the box from firm card. In some cases the frame may need extra support so you will need to reinforce

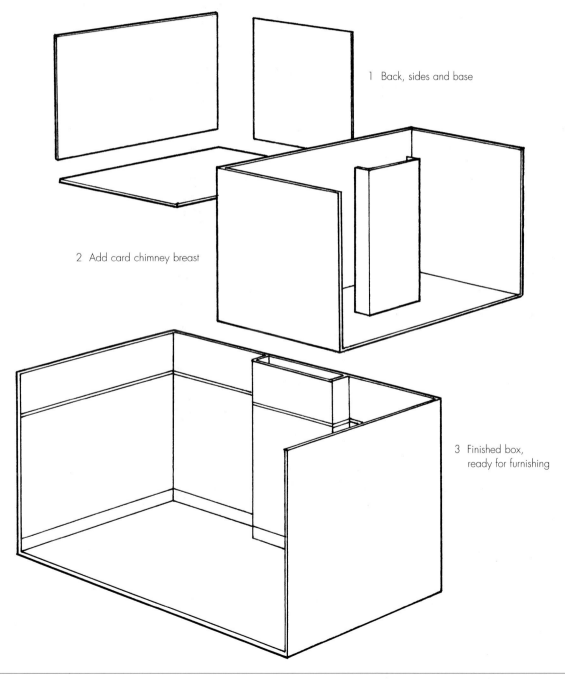

1 Back, sides and base

2 Add card chimney breast

3 Finished box, ready for furnishing

it with strips of card or balsa. For more elaborate items, such as dressers and cabinets, the basic box shape will need to be altered. Examples of this are given later in the book.

Shop fronts

In shop fronts, where a stronger material is needed for the box, I use ⁷⁄₃₂in (6mm) plywood for the base and ⁵⁄₃₂in (4mm) for the walls. A DIY shop will cut pieces to size if you provide them with the dimensions, or you can buy it in sheets. Foamcore is also very good, cuts easily and doesn't warp. It is available in art shops in sheets 20 x 30in (50.5 x 76mm), and in ¹⁄₁₆in (2mm) and ³⁄₁₆in (5mm) thicknesses.

For the lid I like to use clear plastic sheeting. This lets the light into your box and so gives a clearer display of your furniture. All you need do to get sheeting to fit is to score it and crack along the score line.

You may like to extend the base of your box to allow for a pavement display. I always extend the front above the lid so that the box is hidden. Windows and doors can be cut from the front with a fret saw. To fill the frame I like to use flexiglass because it doesn't distort, though clear plastic sheeting also works well.

Create the character of your shop front through the use of decorative trimmings. You may like a balcony with railings. Build one up with card and decorate it with filigree chain links, a bangle opened out, or beads atop card pillars. Stick-on furniture mouldings can be used above doorways and arches and sections of plastic doily look very impressive as a fanlight above a front door. For doorknobs and handles use chain links and beads. Brick paper is an effective covering for a shop front and is very easy to use. Contact, available in a wide range of colours and prints, can be used on floors. If you want hoardings and shop signs, scale size advertisements and lettering are available commercially but you could also cut them from magazines and reduce them to size on a photocopier.

Room settings

Your furniture will be shown to greatest effect when it is in the context of a room. Making a room setting is quite a simple thing to do. If you have a box or frame in which to display your furniture, all you need is firm card and giftwrap. Cut the card to fit the box or frame, then score and bend it to form a back and sides. Now cover the walls with giftwrap to create a mood for the room.

This is the very simplest of room settings. To this you could add a floor with rugs, boards or tiling and you could add cornices, skirting boards, archways and staircases. Vary the setting to suit your particular room. Some of the ways in which I have adapted it can be seen later in the book. I often start with a fireplace built in to the original setting. To do this, score and bend to the shape shown.

5 Corner Shop

I have gradually accumulated various shops and accommodated them on a shelf. I needed a corner shop to finish off the row but the space I had left wasn't large. I started by drawing a ground plan and designed the shop accordingly. I came up with this and as it is such a small box, it has the advantage of being light and portable.

Of course, being small also meant that it didn't have much room for display so the goods it sold had to be tiny. I wanted goods that glittered, so I rejected a sweet shop and tobacconist and chose a clock shop.

Silus Capement hopes to have his own workshop at the back of the shop but I've explained that that would mean a longer shelf (or an arrangement with our neighbours!). He can't sell grandfather clocks but contents himself with ornate clocks which he sells to the carriage trade.

Street lamp

This is really just a pile-up job, though it doesn't start at the bottom. It will help to keep the lamp vertical if you bore a central hole where you can, and thread a thin piece of dowel through them all.

Materials

Tiny jar
Galleried brooch findings
 x 2
Flat button
Bead
Pin
Filigree metal bead cap
Christmas tree light holder
Cake-candle holder
Drinking straw
Long links, filled in x 2
Felt pin lid
Tipp-Ex lid
Phial cap

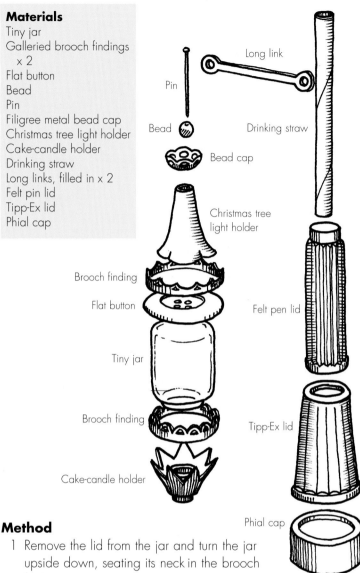

Method

1 Remove the lid from the jar and turn the jar upside down, seating its neck in the brooch finding.
2 Glue the button to the jar for a roof.
3 Glue the second brooch finding in the centre of the button.
4 Pierce the bead with the pin, stick the pin through the bead cap, and then into the Christmas tree light holder. (The top of a tiny chesspiece here would be equally effective.)
5 Glue this in place on the top of the lamp.
6 Glue the lower brooch finding to the cake-candle holder.
7 Cut a hole in both sides of the straw and insert one end of each long link. Glue these in place for added stability.
8 Fit the shaft of the candle holder into the straw.
9 Insert the straw into the felt pen lid.
10 Glue the felt pen lid to the Tipp-Ex lid (it's nicely recessed for this).
11 Glue the Tipp-Ex lid to the phial cap.
12 Mask the jar and the Tipp-Ex lid, and spray the lamp black.

Clockshop counter

A display cabinet is an indispensable part of any clock or jewellery shop. This cabinet could also be used to house any ornaments that you have made, such as vases and perfume bottles.

Materials
Clear plastic sheet
Small plastic box
Picture of stained glass (to fit box)
Card, light
Embossed cake foil strip
Plastic banister rods or
　turned toothpicks

Method

1 Cut one or two pieces of firm, clear plastic to fit box. Glue these in place as shelves on which to display your wares.
2 Carefully glue the picture of the stained glass panel under the lid of the plastic box.
3 Band around the counter top with card, scoring it at the corners to get a good fit.
4 Band around the bottom of the counter with a wider strip of card.
5 Glue the embossed foil strip to bottom band.
6 Glue the banister rods or toothpicks in place to form pillars.
7 Paint all the 'wooden' parts gold/brown.

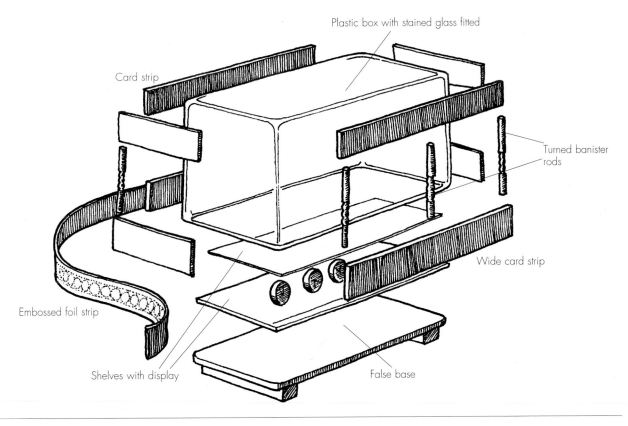

Plastic box with stained glass fitted

Card strip

Turned banister rods

Wide card strip

Embossed foil strip

Shelves with display

False base

Watches and clocks

Watches and clocks are so easy to make! Keep your eye open for any suitable watch faces in catalogues or magazines. The only prerequisite is that the image be straight on. Size is important, but faces can be enlarged or reduced in photocopying.

Method

Watches

1 Reduce the pictures of watch faces to scale size by photocopying.
2 Cut the faces out and mount them on sequins.
3 Attach fine chain to the watch faces for straps.

Clocks

1 Cut out the watch face.
2 Mount the face on chosen item. (I have even used ring pulls from beer cans.)
3 Make a dome to cover the face by cutting down the lipstick cover or phial.

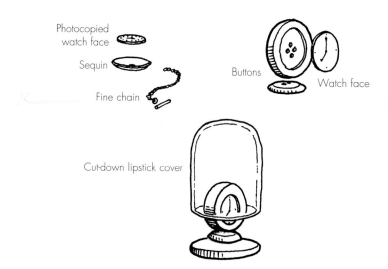

Photocopied watch face

Sequin

Fine chain

Buttons

Watch face

Cut-down lipstick cover

Materials

Watches
Pictures or watch faces
Sequins
Fine chain

Clocks
Picture of watch face
Suitable mount (e.g. card, button, brooch or earring with stone removed, buckle, scarf ring, link)
Clear plastic lipstick cover or phial

Swivel seat

When you buy a drawer handle it comes with a shaft, which gives you all you need for a chair base. Add a back to this and you have a seat!

Materials
Small drawer handle unit
Filigree metal bracelet link

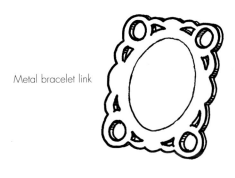

Metal bracelet link

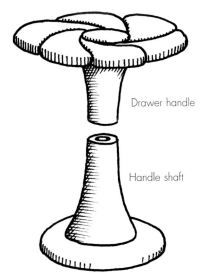

Drawer handle

Handle shaft

Method
1 Attach the drawer handle to the shaft.
2 Glue the bracelet link to the back of the handle.
3 Spray paint all parts.

6 Hall

The character of Sheila Blige's establishment, Nearly Court, demanded a stained glass front door and a stained glass panel halfway up the stairs. Before the room was made, I decided that I wanted to see light through the stained glass panels, so I made a box for the room and a shell to fit inside it, through which light could shine, and which I could remove and display separately. The door panels are commercially printed ones which I coloured in using oil-based overhead projector pens. For the panel I used

a little stained-glass fob I possessed and set it into the shell's side. The arches are made of card and faced with stick-on furniture decorations. The carpet is a quilted top from an old make-up tray and the staircase a run of commercial dolls' house stairs with a larger step added at the bottom. The tread cushions are cuts from postcards of William Morris designs. A set of cocktail forks, cut at an angle and topped with a wooden rail, form the staircase banisters, while for the banisters upstairs, I used cut down lengths of plastic railings.

Hall light

When I found a brooch with three stones, I decided to use it for a hall light as it would give me settings for three bulbs. For an even grander light, use a brooch with six stones.

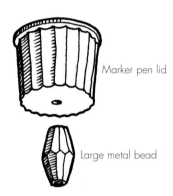

Materials

Brooch, with three or six stones
Christmas tree light holders x 3
Round glass beads x 3
Fluted lid of marker pen
Brass wire
Large metal bead
Belt-hole eyelet
Small metal bead

Marker pen lid

Large metal bead

Eyelet

Wire

Small metal bead

Method

1 Remove the pin and stones from the brooch.
2 Glue the light holders in the stone settings, leaving space between them.
3 Glue a glass bead in each light holder to look like a bulb.
4 Drill a hole in the pen lid and thread the wire through it.
5 Thread onto the wire in turn, the large metal bead, the belt-hole eyelet and the small metal bead.
6 Glue the large bead and eyelet to the top of the wire, immediately under the pen lid.
7 Leave some space between the eyelet and the small bead, trim the wire and glue the bead to the back of the brooch assembly.

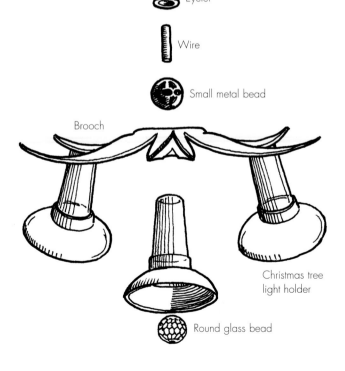

Brooch

Christmas tree light holder

Round glass bead

Hall stand

Hair curlers are extremely versatile makings. Use them here, topped with beads, for pillars to frame the back panel.

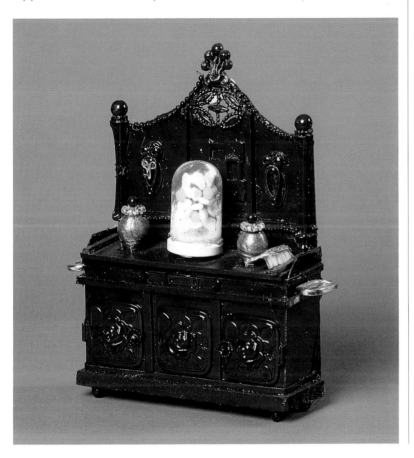

Materials
Card, medium
Card, heavy
Small beads x 4
Square metal bracelet links x 4
Press stud fasteners x 2
Map pins x 2
Small chain link
Brooch
Home perm curlers x 2
Large beads x 2
Ball-and-socket 'bobble' chain
Jewellery finding
Small drop earrings x 2
Hook and eye fasteners
Small curtain rings x 2

Method
1 Use card to make up the box shape, with a high back to fit.
2 Cut a top to fit the box, and another to overlap this.
3 Mount the whole assembly on a card base.
4 Stand the base on four bead feet.
5 Arrange bracelet links at intervals to make decorative doors on the front.
6 Stick press stud fasteners to the outer doors for handles.
7 Use strips of card to make panels on the back.
8 Glue a bracelet link at the base of the centre panel on the back.
9 Place a brooch above this link, trace around it, and cut this shape out. Mount the brooch over this hole, to give a see through effect.
10 Use a drop earring to decorate each side panel.
11 Make columns at either side of the hall stand, from home perm curlers topped with a bead.
12 Run bobble chain along the top and base of the back to trim.

13 Crown pediment with a jewellery finding.
14 Make bars with strips of card, between and across the top of
   the panels on the front, and across the hall stand's sides.
15 Spray paint brown.
16 Attach hooks from hook and eye fasteners to drop earrings.
17 Fix the small chain link to the centre top of the front as a
   maker's nameplate, and stick a pin at either side of this.
18 Add squashed curtain rings to the sides for umbrella rests.

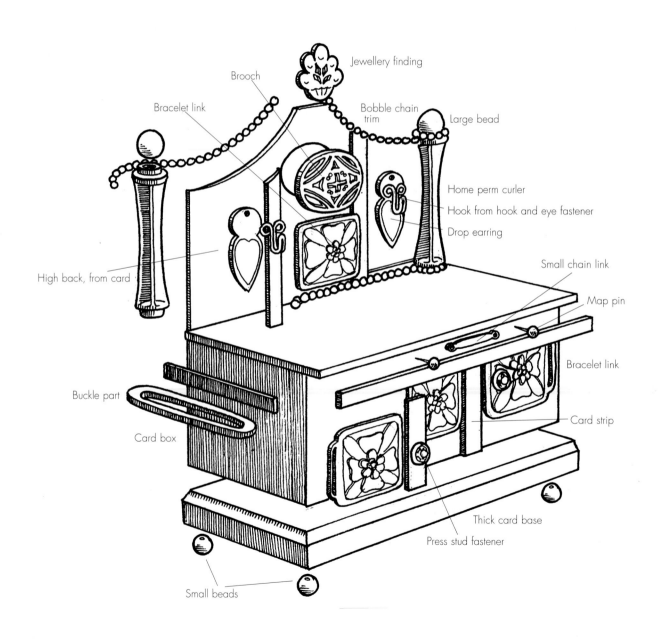

Hat stand

This uses a fish-hook on which to hang the hats. Please be very careful handling it, and keep out of reach of children – the barbs are very sharp!

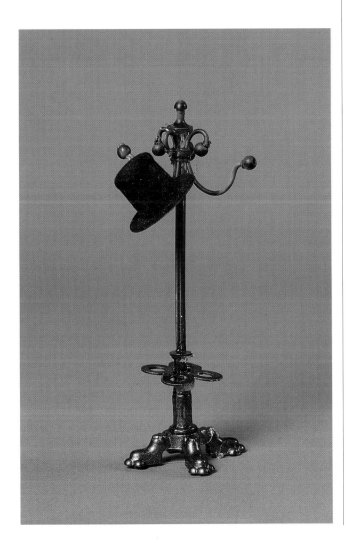

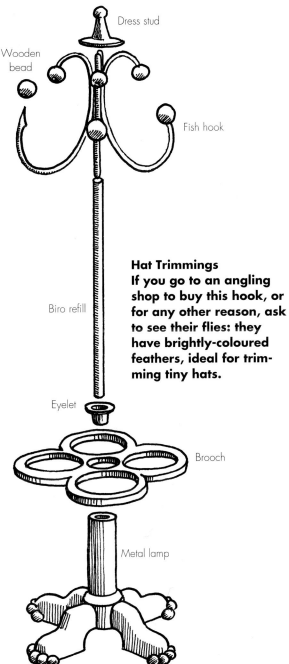

Hat Trimmings
If you go to an angling shop to buy this hook, or for any other reason, ask to see their flies: they have brightly-coloured feathers, ideal for trimming tiny hats.

Materials

Miniature metal lamp
Brooch, or some other item with a central hole
Belt-hole eyelet
Metal Biro refill
Wooden beads with large holes
Fish-hook
Dress stud

Method

1 Cut the feet off the metal lamp, and thread this through the centre of the brooch or whatever you have chosen to use.
2 Glue the eyelet into the centre of the brooch, to house the pole made from the Biro refill.
3 Very carefully wedge a bead onto each barb of the fish-hook.
4 Mount the hook, safely diffused with beads, onto the top of the pole.
5 Top this with the dress stud.
6 Spray paint gold.

Hall table

Really, this is just a collection of drop earrings, without which it would be featureless. So, if you are a jumble sale addict, look out for these! I could not believe my eyes when I was offered just one metal drop earring in the form of a column – you may have the other one! If you can't find a column earring, use a wedding-cake column instead.

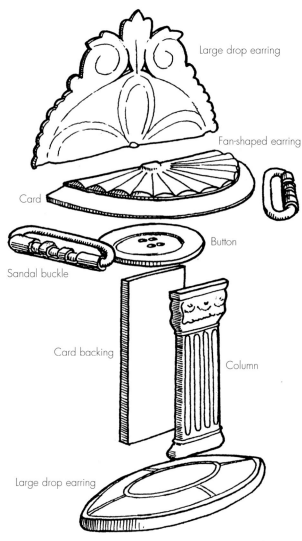

Large drop earring

Fan-shaped earring

Card

Sandal buckle

Button

Card backing

Column

Large drop earring

Method
1 Reinforce the column with the card.
2 Glue this to one of the large drop earrings.
3 Glue the button to the top of the column. This makes a base for the table top.
4 Use the fan-shaped earring as the table top. Glue it onto the button.
5 Glue the sandal buckles to either side of the table top to take umbrellas or walking sticks.
6 Back the table with the other large drop earring and glue it in place.

Umbrellas
Umbrellas and walking sticks can be made by bending slender knitting needles in hot water and cutting them to size.

Materials
Card, heavy
Column of some sort
Large drop earrings x 2
Button
Fan-shaped earring
Sandal buckles x 2

7 Pub

To create the atmosphere of a pub, I wanted my bar to be warm and bright, so I used paper with a bold design and strong colours to cover the walls, and filled the room with photos and plants to give a homely atmosphere.

To add sparkle, I hung a row of crystal beads across the bar and used a mirror to back the bar shelves. These are even more effective with lights in your room.

Pub bar

To sketch the bar, I had to go to the pub! I recommend you do the same (even if you forget to sketch!) The closest I could come to approximating the fancy glass rack, was to use some plastic railing I had picked up at a dolls' house shop, so that had to do. Of course, they look nothing like the original, but what I'm after is atmosphere rather than accuracy.

Materials

Bar
Card
Turned dolls' house banister rods
    (commercial)
Cocktail forks
Metal washers
Toothpaste lids
Fancy plastic dolls' house railing
    (commercial)
Fancy plastic picture frame
Solid metal link (e.g. from belt or chain)
Fancy beads
Bead caps
Three-into-one necklace clasps
'Crystal' beads

Method

Bar
1 Make up box shape from card (mine is L-shaped), and fit a base and top to this.
2 Glue card panels across the front.
3 Cut a second card piece the same shape as the bar.
4 Seat the banister rods in the metal washers, fix the toothpaste lids to their tops, and glue these in place across the top of the bar.
5 Mount the bar-shaped card on these, to form a shelf above the bar.
6 Run the plastic railing all around this high shelf.
7 Decorate the front of the shelf with fancy picture frame.
8 Finish off each end with a cocktail fork handle.
9 Block in both ends of the bar, to the top, with card panels.
10 Decorate the tops of these panels with cocktail forks cut to size.
11 Spray paint.
12 Mount three cocktail fork handles on metal washers, then glue these to a small metal plate, for pump handles.

13 Glue fancy beads to bead caps, and mount these on
   necklace clasps to make lights. Fix these to the top shelf.
14 Hang crystal beads below the top shelf for 'twinkle factor'.
15 Trim around the base of the bar front with card.

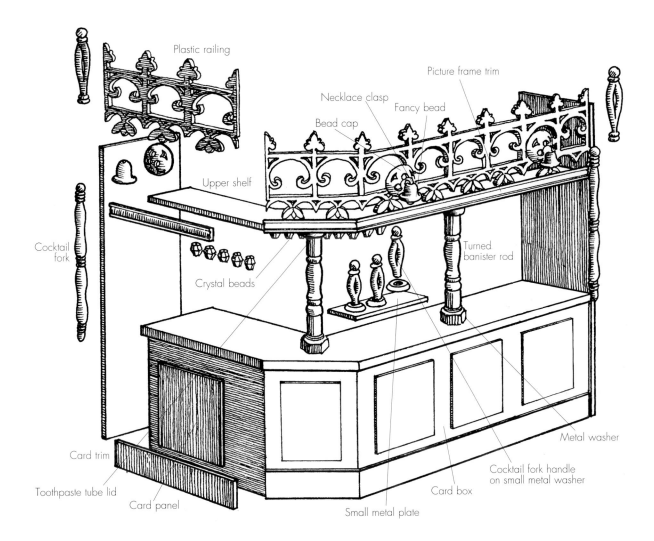

Glasses
**If you need lots of
glasses, you can use
short lengths cut from
Biro casing, clear straws,
or clear plastic tubing.
Of course, they have no
bottoms but it doesn't
show. You can also use
cut glass beads which
look like tumblers.
Handles can be made
from chain links cut in
half.**

Picture Frames
**Use earrings, brooches
or small buckles to make
these. Remove the central
stones and replace them
with tiny pictures. You
can reduce the size of
photos, or pictures cut
from magazines, on a
photocopier.**

Vases
**Look out for interesting
large beads, and use
flat beads, tiny washers,
watch winders, sequins
and bead caps to build
them into elaborate
shapes.**

Method

Bar Shelves

1 Cut shelves from the balsa to the same size, or of varying lengths.
2 Glue these onto the mirror.
3 Use straws, cut to size, to form pillars.
4 Trim the top of the mirror by running plastic railing along it.
5 For glasses along the shelves, use cuts of plastic pipe. I used some commercial dolls' house bottles on my shelves, interspersed with medicine bottles, and even the odd photo.

Materials

Bar Shelves
Balsa
Small mirror
Plastic railing
Drinking straws
Plastic pipe

Plastic railing

Balsa shelf

Mirror

Pillars cut
from straw

Potted Palm Shelves
These are so easy! Just open up clip-on earrings, and glue the clip to the wall. The earring itself becomes the shelf. I stuck a little jewellery bow on the front, but it looks good plain as well.

Clip-on earring

Jewellery bow

Soda syphon

The Sectzogen Clincher soda water syphon (c.1890) looks rather like Sheila Blige to me, so it seemed fitting that her bar be equipped with one. It's not exactly essential to the average dolls' house, but it would be an invaluable extra and give a touch of class. Making the basic syphon shape is a pile-up job, so it is best to first pierce the objects and thread them onto a central post for stability and ease of construction.

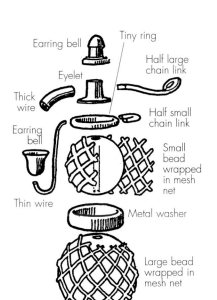

Materials

Small mesh net
Clear glass beads x 2, one smaller than the other
Flat metal button
Metal washers x 2
Tiny ring (e.g. as found between necklace beads)
Belt-hole eyelet
Earring bells x 2
Large chain link x ½
Thick wire
Thin wire
Small round chain link x ½

Method

1   Glue a small cylinder of net around each glass bead and tuck the net in at the top and bottom so that the beads are completely covered.
2   Now the pile-up begins! In order, pile the flat metal button (for the base), one of the metal washers, the larger netted bead, the second washer, the smaller netted bead, the tiny ring, the eyelet and one of the earring bells.
3   For the handle, glue the large chain link in place.
4   Bend a piece of the thick wire and glue it opposite the handle for the spout.
5   Glue the small chain link below the handle.
6   Bend another piece of the wire and attach the other earring bell to this.
7   Glue the wire to the syphon, opposite the small chain link.

Pub bench

Using graduated bracelet links for this bench gives a gentle curve to its back.

Materials

Filigree metal link bracelet with
  graduated links
Card
Cocktail forks x 2
Balsa block
Triangular moulding strip (commercial)
Old velvet (new velvet is too inflexible)
Wadding
Lampshade gimp

Method

1 Cut a back from the card that will accommodate the four largest bracelet links and reach to the ground.
2 Glue the four links to the upper part of the back.
3 Cut and fit card strips to trim above and below the links.
4 Cut the handles off the cocktail forks and use them for posts at both ends of the bench back.
5 Cut and shape the balsa to form the seat.
6 Cut two short lengths of the triangular strip to form legs. Glue them to the base of the seat.
7 Cut a piece of card to form the seat top. Do not glue this in place yet.
8 Spray paint the couch, but not the card seat.
9 Cut a piece of wadding to fit the card seat and a piece of velvet slightly larger than this.
10 Place the wadding on the card and lay the velvet over this.
11 Make small cuts along all sides of the velvet, towards the card, and glue the strips of material to the reverse side of the card.
12 Glue the upholstered seat into place.
13 Run a piece of the lampshade gimp along the balsa block below the upholstered seat.
14 Glue two of the smaller links to each side of the bench, for arms.

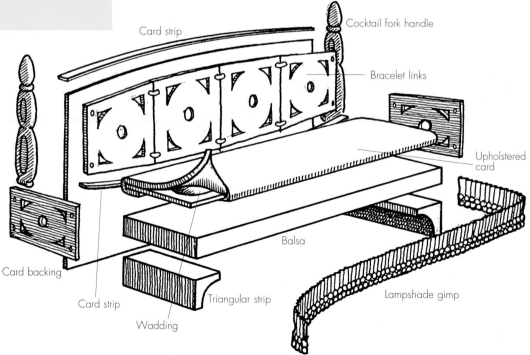

Card strip

Cocktail fork handle

Bracelet links

Upholstered card

Card backing

Card strip

Wadding

Triangular strip

Balsa

Lampshade gimp

Piano

I like the look of pianos with decorative fronts and lamp holders, so that is the style I wanted to make. I used bracelet links for panels and added watch winders and strips of card for decoration. For lamps, I glued bell-shaped beads to jewellery findings.

Method

Piano

1 Cut the two sides from heavy card and the front and back from light card.
2 Before you make up the box shape, arrange the bracelet links as panels on the piano front.
3 Make up the box.
4 Fit a panel of card across the top.
5 Use strips of card to sit at the sides and across the base of each panel.
6 Decorate the strips on the upper part of the piano with watch winders, or small bead caps.
7 Cut a shelf from the balsa to fit the curve of the side panel, and insert this half way up the piano front.
8 Reinforce this with heavy card, and fit the triangular strip above it.
9 Fix strips of card to the sides of the piano, across the top, middle and bottom.
10 Glue a card panel across the base of the piano front, then add a second, thinner panel across the base of this.
11 Spray paint.
12 Make lamps by placing the bell-shaped beads in bead caps.
13 Attach the jewellery findings to each side of the piano for lamp holders, and the tiny link to the front of the piano for a maker's nameplate.
14 For the foot pedals, cut the long link in half and bend into shape.

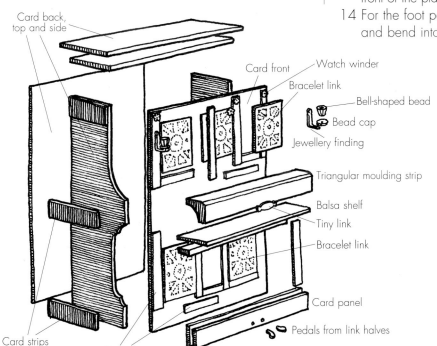

Card back, top and side
Card front
Watch winder
Bracelet link
Bell-shaped bead
Bead cap
Jewellery finding
Triangular moulding strip
Balsa shelf
Tiny link
Bracelet link
Card panel
Pedals from link halves
Card strips
Card strips

Materials

Piano
Card, firm
Card, light
Square bracelet links x 5
Watch winders or small bead caps
Balsa block
Triangular moulding strip
Jewellery findings
Bell-shaped beads
Bead caps
Tiny decorative chain link
Long solid chain link

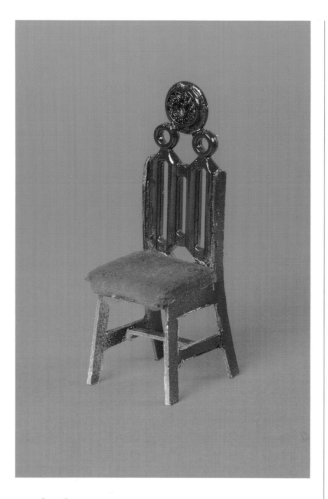

Materials

Piano Chair
Card
Wadding
Fabric
Rectangular filigree link
Flat button
Curtain ring, to fit button

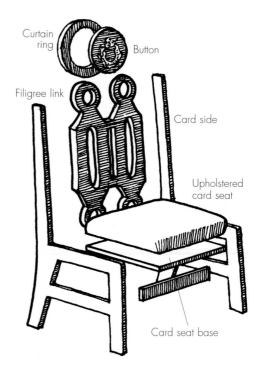

Method

Piano Chair

1 Cut the sides, stile and two seats from the card.
2 Cut a piece of wadding to fit one of the seats.
3 Cut a piece of material slightly larger than the wadding.
4 Place the wadding on the card and lay the material over the wadding.
5 Make little cuts, towards the card, along all sides of the material.
6 Glue the strips of material to the reverse side of the card.
7 Assemble the chair, fitting the link, stile and plain card seat between the two sides.
8 Frame the button in the curtain ring and glue it to the top of the back rest.
9 Spray paint brown.
10 Glue the upholstered seat in place when the paint is dry.

8 Billiard Room

The first thing I made in this room was the fireplace. I filled a metal picture frame with card and cut an opening at the bottom for the grate which I contained in a miniature frame. I cut a back from card, higher than the level of the fireplace, and made shelves with a mirror inset to sit across this.

Early radiators were often hidden behind grills and I needed a set of matching panels for these. I was lucky enough to find a chain belt with lots of identical links. I used these to represent wrought iron and set them in cardboard cupboards. I used a placemat for the rug. There are some very nice ones around and I found a velvet one trimmed with silk that was just the right size.

Billiard table

For the legs of this table, I topped fluted beads with toothpaste lids, and glued the beads to mini pawns. This not only gave an interesting shape, but also gave the solid appearance billiard table legs have.

Method

Table Top

1 Cut a rectangle from the firm card, 10cm (4in) x 16cm (6in).
2 Place the curtain rings on the table top, in the appropriate positions for the pockets, so that they are only half resting on the table.
3 Trace around the half of the ring that is lying on the table.
4 Remove the rings and cut out the half circles that you have traced onto the table. This is to allow access to the pockets.
5 Cut each of the rings in half. Only half of each ring will be used in the construction of the table.
6 Cover the table top with the green baize.
7 Cut four long strips from the firm card, 1 cm (3/8in) wide, to act as cushions.
8 Cut these to fit the table top, allowing access to all of the pockets.
9 Cover the strips with green baize, and glue them into place.
10 If there are any exposed edges on the strips or table, paint them green.
11 Glue the half curtain rings into place, to form the outside edges of the pockets.
12 Bind a strip of the light card around the entire table.

Materials

Table Top
Card, firm
Small plastic curtain rings x 6
Green baize, Fablon or felt
Card, light
Woodgrain Fablon, dark
Net (I used the net from spring curlers)
Balsa strip

Table Legs
Toothpaste tube lids x 4
Fluted beads x 4
Mini pawns x 4

13 Cover this with a strip of the wood grain Fablon, cut to fit.
14 Stiffen the net by spraying it with paint.
15 Wrap the stiffened net around a rod that is a bit thicker than the holes of the pockets.
16 Glue the sides of the net together to form a cylinder, taking care not to stick the net to the rod.
17 Slip the resulting cylinder off the rod, and cut it into six pieces of equal length.
18 Fix each piece of net into the ring of a pocket, and seal their ends.
19 Glue the strip of balsa underneath the table, to reinforce it.

Table Legs

1 For each leg, use a toothpaste lid and a bead, and then glue this to a mini pawn. My table has four legs, but you may prefer six.
2 Glue each leg in place under the table top.
3 It should now be possible to turn the table upside down to spray it brown, though some touching up may be necessary.

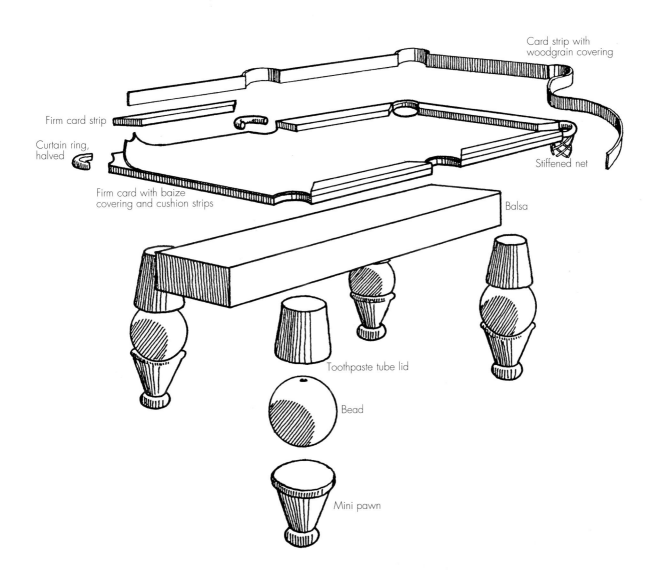

Card strip with woodgrain covering

Firm card strip

Curtain ring, halved

Stiffened net

Firm card with baize covering and cushion strips

Balsa

Toothpaste tube lid

Bead

Mini pawn

Billiard light

Beads and bead caps are the main ingredient here. You can change the appearance of the light by the order and shape of the beads you use.

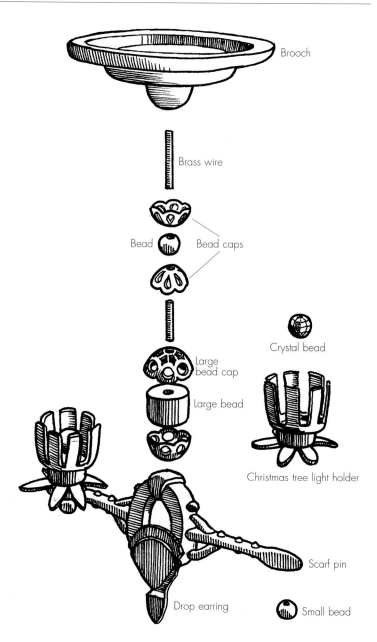

Method

1 Remove the stone from the centre of the scarf pin and glue the drop earring in the space created, to dangle below it.

2 Glue a Christmas tree light holder to both ends of the brooch's 'arms', facing up. You may need a washer to get it to sit well.

3 Use the brooch as a ceiling rose. Drill a central hole in it and thread the wire through.

4 Thread beads and bead caps at intervals along this wire, ending with a large bead and bead cap.

5 Attach the centre of the scarf pin to the beaded wire by bending the arms of the last bead cap around it, to form a clasp.

6 You may like to glue a crystal bead into each light holder, for a bulb, and small beads below the light holders for decoration.

Materials

Long, fancy scarf pin
Drop earring
Christmas tree light holders x 2
Washers x 2 (optional)
Brooch
Brass wire
Beads of various sizes
Bead caps of various sizes
Crystal beads x 2 (optional)

Billiard cue holder

The spokes to hold the billiard cues are from the centre of a plastic doily. You will need one that has a centre that can be cut to produce open 'v's.

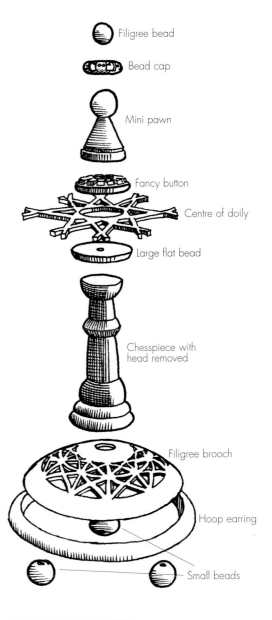

Filigree bead

Bead cap

Mini pawn

Fancy button

Centre of doily

Large flat bead

Chesspiece with head removed

Filigree brooch

Hoop earring

Small beads

Method

1 Frame the brooch with the hoop earring, cutting it to fit if necessary, and glue it in place.
2 Mount the brooch on the three small beads, to form feet.
3 Cut the head off the large chesspiece and glue the base of the chesspiece onto the centre of the brooch.
4 Top the chesspiece with the large, flat bead.
5 Cut the centre out of the doily, so that the open edges are v-shaped.
6 Stick this centre onto the flat bead.
7 Glue the button onto the centre of the doily.
8 Continue up the pile, adding the pawn to the button.
9 Glue the bead cap to the pawn, and finally, the filigree bead to its cap.
10 Spray paint brown. I used metallic paint for its nice shine.

Materials
Filigree brooch
Hoop earring
Small flat beads x 3
Large chesspiece
Large flat bead
Plastic doily
Fancy button
Mini pawn
Bead cap
Filigree bead

**Billiard Cues
Use kebab sticks cut to size, or toothpicks, for billiard cues.**

Fireguard

Use rectangular links for the decoration on this fireguard. They give a more solid appearance to the finished piece.

Method

1 Cut the bangle, and open it out to straighten it. This is not easy but, with a bit of determination and perseverance, it can be done!

2 Bend the bangle to the shape of a fender.

3 Place the bracelet on the card and trace around it. Neaten the outline, and cut out three pieces of card to this shape. The first will be used to form the base, the second for the top of the fireguard, and the third for the leather seat, if you want one.

4 Cut across the middle of one of the zoo fences, and trim off any bobbles.

5 Cut off any ornamentation from the top of the other two fences, which will be used at full height.

6 Measure the metal links against the full-height fencing and, allowing one or two upright rails to frame them on either side, bend the rails around to form fireguard sides.

7 Place the links in position behind the railings, and cut away any rails that cross them, so that they are framed by bars.

8 Fit the top piece of card by cutting away the middle section to fit the half-height fence. Keep the three pieces thus gained.

9 When all your pieces are cut to fit, glue the fireguard frame to the base, stick the top and middle sections on, and fix the links in their frames.

10 Drape the bangle around the base, and glue it in place. This strengthens the fireguard and gives it an added touch of realism.

11 Use the necklace clasp to the front as a centre detail.

12 Attach the two chain links to the top, inside rails, for decoration and for reinforcing.

13 Add toothpicks to each of the corners, front and back.

14 Spray paint brown.

15 If you do want a seat top, cut the middle out of the remaining card and upholster the two outside pieces, using the Leatherette.

16 When they are dry, stick the upholstered seats onto the top rails.

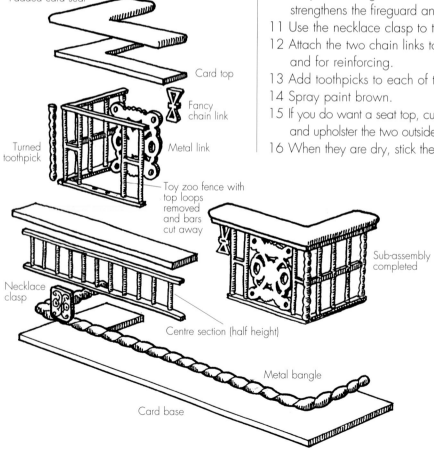

Padded card seat

Card top

Fancy chain link

Turned toothpick

Metal link

Toy zoo fence with top loops removed and bars cut away

Sub-assembly completed

Necklace clasp

Centre section (half height)

Metal bangle

Card base

Materials

Narrow, metal bangle
Card
Plastic toy zoo fence x 3
Rectangular metal links (belt or bracelet) x 2
Small necklace clasp
Fancy chain links x 2
Toothpicks x 4
Leatherette (e.g. from an old diary: optional)

Comb couch

Use embroidery silk and lampshade gimp to create a rich look for this couch.

Materials

Fancy haircomb
Card, heavy
Card, light
Balsa block, 1in (25.5mm) wide
Filigree plastic fan (a small
    section will do)
Wadding or cotton wool
Old velvet (new velvet is too
    inflexible)
Embroidery silk
Lampshade gimp

Method

1 Holding the comb upright, trace around it onto the heavy card.
2 Extend this tracing forward to form a seat pattern, and cut this out.
3 Trace around your seat pattern onto light card, and cut this out. This will be upholstered later.
4 Once again, trace around your seat pattern, this time onto the balsa, and cut the seat base from this.
5 Glue the ends of the comb's teeth along the back of the balsa base, curving the comb around as the glue dries. (If you use a glue gun to do this, the hot glue is strong enough to hold the comb in place despite the curve.)
6 Select curlicues from the fan to fill in spaces at the ends of the comb, if there are any.
7 Spray paint.
8 Cut some wadding or cotton wool to the shape of the seat.
9 Cut the velvet to the shape of the seat, leaving a margin of about ½in (12mm) so that it overhangs all around.
10 Lay the wadding on the reverse side of the velvet. Don't try to stick the wadding down: it doesn't mix well with glue! The velvet will eventually hold it in place.
11 Place the light card upside down on the wadding and velvet.

12 Fold and glue the straight side of the velvet onto the underside of the card.
13 Make little cuts in the velvet, towards the card, at ¼in (6mm) intervals, all
   around the remaining three sides. Now you can glue these pieces of velvet
   down, without getting too many lumps.
14 Trim any spare velvet.
15 Turn the upholstered seat the right way up, and glue it to the heavy card.
16 Use the spare velvet and wadding to make a pillow.
17 Make two tassels. To do this, wind the embroidery silk around your finger, cut
   it at one end and bind it at the other, a little below the top, with more thread.
18 Attach one tassel to each end of the pillow.
19 Disguise the balsa by gluing the gimp across it.
20 Decorate the top of the comb with another strip of gimp.

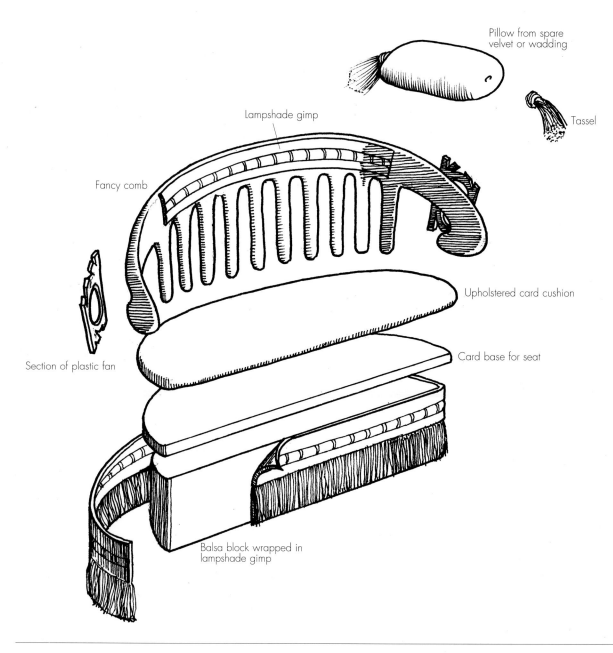

Pillow from spare velvet or wadding

Tassel

Lampshade gimp

Fancy comb

Upholstered card cushion

Section of plastic fan

Card base for seat

Balsa block wrapped in lampshade gimp

Coal box

Make up the shape of this coal box from card, and add character through its decorations. Use a bracelet link or any other findings that you have to hand.

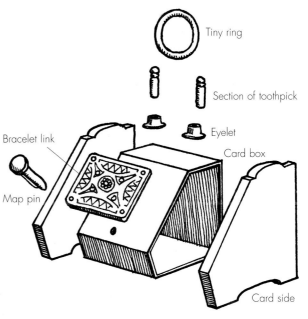

Template for box

Front	Top	Back	Bottom

Materials
Card, medium
Card, heavy
Fancy square bracelet link
Turned toothpicks x 2
Belt-hole eyelets x 2
Tiny ring (e.g. as found between necklace beads)
Map pin

Method
1. Cut the long piece shown in the diagram from the medium card.
2. Cut the sides, illustrated, from the heavy card.
3. Score the long piece as shown, and bend it to form a box shape with a sloped front.
4. Glue the two side pieces in place.
5. Decorate the front of the box with the bracelet link, and glue it in place.
6. Insert the pin into the front of the box, below the link.
7. Cut the toothpicks short, and insert each of the pieces you are using into an eyelet.
8. Mount these on top of the box at the correct width to hold the ring, to make a handle.
9. Spray paint.

Welsh dresser

I was lucky enough to find some particularly elaborate bracelet links for this, but with simple links, the dresser will look impressive just the same!

Materials

Card, medium
Large metal rectangular
    bracelet links x 3
Small metal rectangular
    bracelet links x 3
Card, light
Small beads x 4
Small bead caps x 4
Large beads x 2
Large bead caps x 4
Stick-on furniture decoration
Jewellery pieces (e.g. links,
    bead caps)
Circular link
Small chain links x 2
Tiny gold beads x 2
Pewter plates (commercial)

Method

1 Cut back, sides, front, base and shelves from the medium card.
2 Score along dotted lines on the back panel, and bend to make the dresser's sides.
3 Arrange the bracelet links on the front to look like doors and drawers.
4 Cut strips of light card to panel across the front.
5 Glue the front in place between the side panels.

6 Attach the base, and mount the dresser on four bead feet with bead caps.

7 Insert shelves at intervals, with a larger one to top the dresser front. Support the shelf above with beads and bead caps, piled up.

8 Top the whole dresser with a lid, and face it with a baffle.

9 Decorate the baffle with the stick-on furniture decorations.

10 Spray paint before adding gold beads and links for drawer and cupboard handles.

11 Arrange the plates on the shelves.

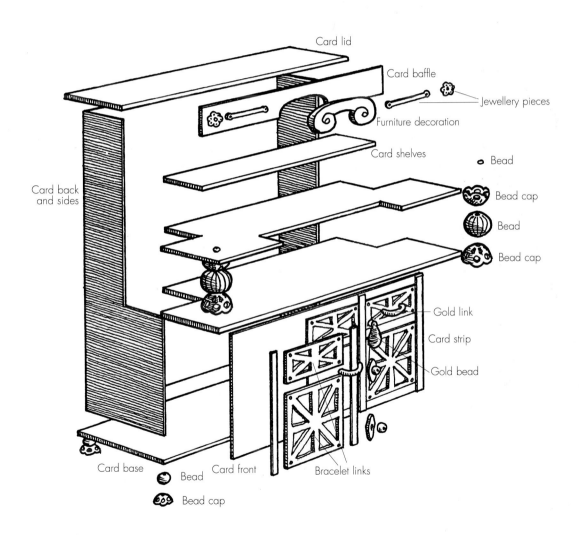

Reservoir lamp

This may look complicated, but it can be made simply, in three separate parts.

Method

Reservoir

1 Sandwich the cartridge between two metal washers.
2 Top this with an eyelet and a bead.
3 Attach the other eyelet to the middle of the cartridge.

Lamp

1 Fix the eyelet to the side of the small dress stud, making a pad of glue to seat it on.
2 Mount the glass bead in the bead cap to form the lamp, and place this on the top of the dress stud.
3 Make the lampshade from the button, gluing the screw-hole cover to its underside, and the button, upside down, to the glass bead.
4 Use a short piece of clear plastic straw, or Biro refill, to the top of the screw-hole cover for the funnel.

Stand

1 Attach the large dress stud to the brass button.
2 Glue the small, flat metal bead to the top of the dress stud.
3 Attach a round metal bead to each end of the brass wire.
4 Stick one of these beads to the flat bead.
5 Glue the necklace fastener to the top bead.
6 Attach the reservoir to one of the stud's arms by sticking the eyelet to it.
7 Attach the lamp to the other arm in the same way.

Materials

Reservoir
Metal washers x 2
Small metal cartridge case
Belt-hole eyelets x 2
Small metal bead

Lamp
Small dress stud
Belt-hole eyelet
Large glass bead
Large bead cap
White button
DIY screw-hole cover
Clear plastic straw or Biro refill

Stand
Large dress stud
Brass button (same shape as dress stud)
Small flat metal bead
Small round metal beads x 2
Brass wire
Necklace fastener, screw type

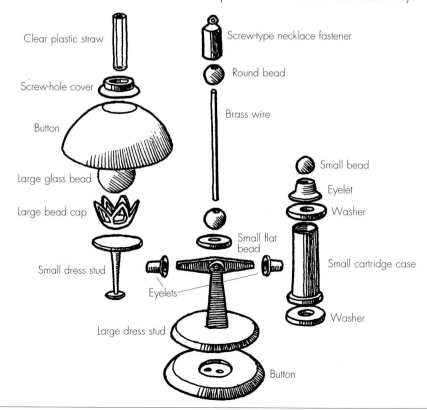

Clear plastic straw

Screw-type necklace fastener

Screw-hole cover

Round bead

Button

Brass wire

Large glass bead

Large bead cap

Small bead

Eyelet

Washer

Small dress stud

Small flat bead

Small cartridge case

Eyelets

Large dress stud

Washer

Button

Oil lamp

Another pile-up job! This lamp is very simple to make.

Materials
Brass button
Brass washer
Gold bead
Belt-hole eyelet
Large bead cap
Glass bead
Small bead cap
Clear plastic straw
Watch winder
Tiny bead cap

Method

1 Turn the button upside down and onto it glue, in this order, the washer, gold bead, eyelet, large bead cap, glass bead, small bead cap, and a short length of the plastic straw.
2 Thread the watch winder through the tiny bead cap and attach this to the side of the gold bead.

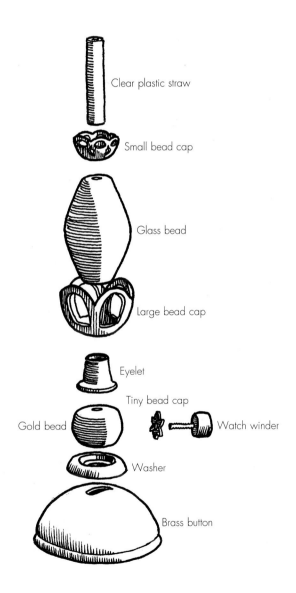

Clear plastic straw

Small bead cap

Glass bead

Large bead cap

Eyelet

Tiny bead cap

Gold bead

Watch winder

Washer

Brass button

Easy table

You've heard of easy chairs, this is an easy table! Make several as gifts.

Materials
Chesspiece
Small flat button
Buckle
Large flat button

Decoration
Use a bowl of ferns, photo or potted plant to cover the button holes.

Method
1   Glue the chesspiece to the small button.
2   File the top of the chesspiece flat.
3   Cut the centre bar out of the buckle, and fill the space created with the large button.
4   Spray paint.

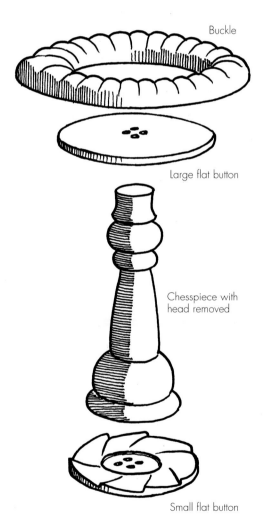

Buckle

Large flat button

Chesspiece with head removed

Small flat button

9 Hummer Peacock Room

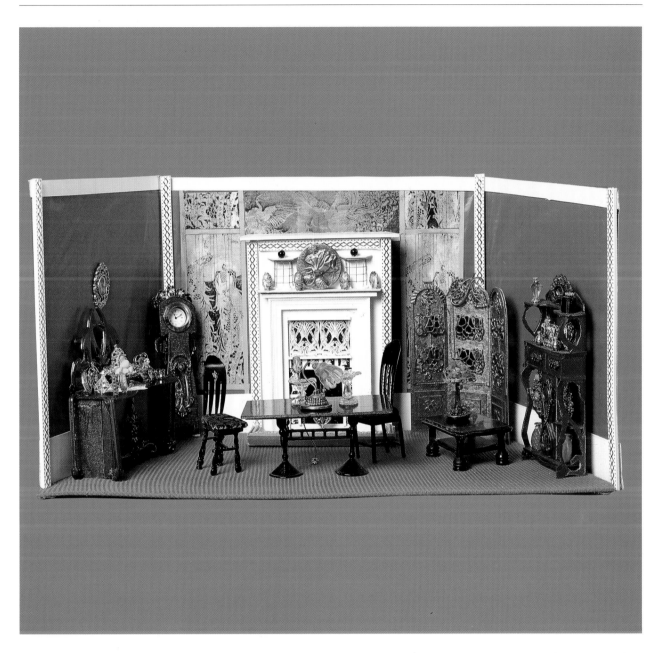

The Hummer Peacock Room, with its bold and innovative interior in the Art Nouveau style, was especially designed for Sheila Blige by Alto Hummer, in recognition of all she had done for him.

The two met when Al was a struggling young artist, newly arrived from the USA and living in London, painting foggy watercolours of the Thames. Sheila became his model, and the liaison went on into old age when Hummer painted perhaps his best known picture of her, posing, fully clad, on a couch. The work, full length and in unusually restrained tones, achieved a measure of success. It is known simply as Portrait of Hummer's Mother: a misnomer, of course.

The Hummer Room was later bought in its entirety by the Freer Museum and can be seen there, though in a slightly altered form. It is considered one of Hummer's finest achievements.

Art Nouveau fireplace

In order to get an authentic look, I found some William Morris design giftwrap and some illustrations of tiles I liked, and reduced both to the size I required on a photocopier. That gave me the tiles and patterns I needed, but all in white, so the colour of the fireplace was set.

Method

1 Carefully remove the card backing from the bubble pack. This should be the right shape for the hearth.
2 Spray paint black.
3 Cut the bottom off the door frame.
4 Cut a piece of card to fit inside the remaining frame.
5 Cut a rectangle out of the card to house the fire, and fit the sprayed bubble pack behind this.
6 Decorate the surround with the tiles and giftwrap design.
7 Cut a piece of balsa to form a shelf, and glue this to the top of the fireplace. Top this with a slightly larger piece of card.
8 Cut another piece of card, taller than the door frame and to the width of the picture frame. Glue the entire assembly to this, cutting a rectangle from the card to house the bubble pack if necessary.
9 Glue the moulding across the top and down the sides.
10 Cut another shelf from balsa and glue this across the top of the larger frame.
11 Cut two small squares from the wire mesh and bend them to form a front and two narrow sides.
12 Mount each mesh box on the lower shelf, leaving enough space between them to fit the brooch. If you want feet, glue small white beads at each of the corners, and trim the centre wires in the mesh.
13 Top each box with a shaped piece of card, as shown in the diagram. You may like to top this with a larger shaped card for extra detail.
14 Mount the two round beads on the tops of the boxes.

15 Glue the brooch between the boxes.
16 Arrange the cylindrical beads across the bottom shelf, as vases.
17 Cut the picture frame down to use as a hearth and glue it to the fireplace assembly.
18 Cut a piece of card to fill the hearth and fix it in place.
19 Decorate the hearth step with tiles.
20 Use the second brooch as a fireguard.

Materials

Balsa
Rectangular bubble pack, clear
Dolls' house door frame (commercial)
Card, heavy
Tiles
Giftwrap (e.g. William Morris design)
Stick-on moulding
Large wire mesh
Small white beads x 8 (optional)
Brooches x 2
Round beads x 2
Cylindrical beads
Small picture frame

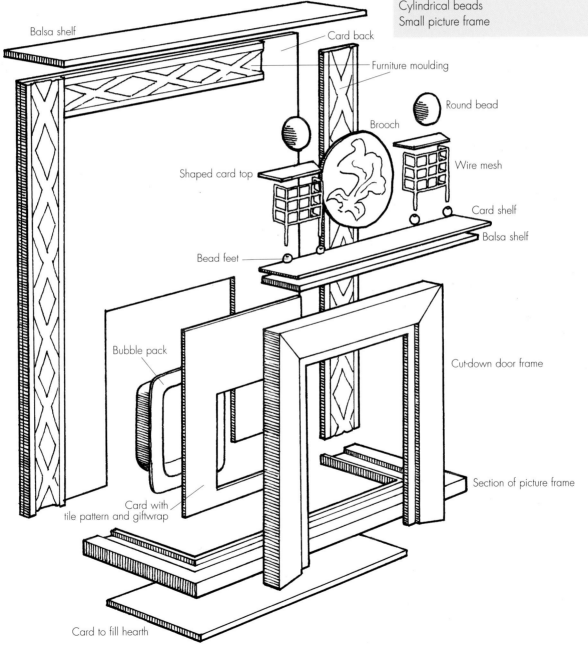

Balsa shelf

Card back

Furniture moulding

Round bead

Brooch

Shaped card top

Wire mesh

Card shelf

Balsa shelf

Bead feet

Bubble pack

Cut-down door frame

Section of picture frame

Card with
tile pattern and giftwrap

Card to fill hearth

Coffee table

Belt buckles give this coffee table its distinctive shape, and the black finish adds to its elegance.

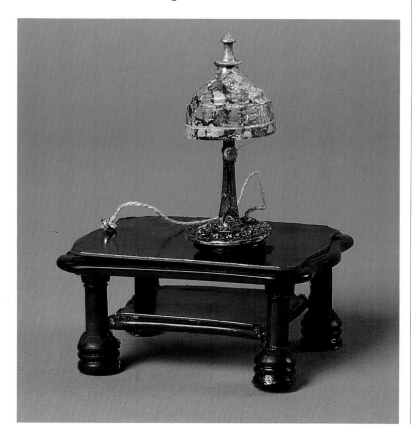

Method

1 Trace around both buckles onto the card and cut their shapes out.
2 Trim the pieces of card so that they are a little smaller than their respective buckles.
3 Top each buckle with the appropriate piece of card.
4 Glue a chesspiece under each corner of the large buckle, with the correct spacing to fit the small buckle between them.
5 Insert and glue the small buckle between the chesspiece legs to form a shelf.
6 Spray paint black.

Materials

Large rectangular buckle
Small rectangular buckle
Card, medium
Chesspieces x 4

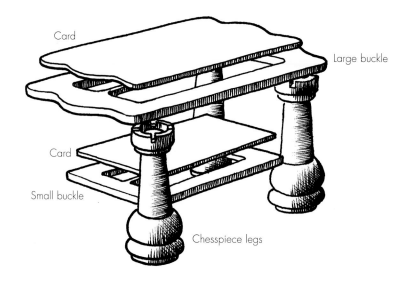

Card

Large buckle

Card

Small buckle

Chesspiece legs

Dining table

A few years ago there was a great craze for brass miniatures of old time gramophones, kettles, lampshades . . . that sort of thing. Now they can be found at jumble sales for a few pence each. They are nicely made, though too big to use in the dolls' house. However, I realized that the three-pronged candlesticks would make nice table supports and used them for just that.

Materials

Card, heavy
Three-armed miniature
    candlesticks x 2 (commercial)
Miniature ladder, gauge o
    (commercial)

Method

1   Cut a rectangle from the card to the size you want for the table top.
2   Cut the middle candle cup off both candlesticks.
3   Glue the candlesticks to the underside of the table top.
4   Glue a short length of the ladder between the candlesticks.
5   Spray paint black.

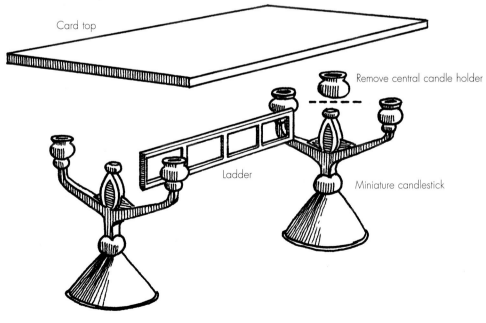

Card top

Remove central candle holder

Ladder

Miniature candlestick

Art Nouveau lamps

I have just found out that it is possible to find replacement pourers for saltcellars. This is good news not only for salt addicts, but for modellers too because they are the perfect shape for Tiffany lampshades. You can paint plastic with water colours if you first drag your paintbrush over a bar of soap. This breaks up the surface tension and stops the paint from blobbing. When the paint is dry, varnish it carefully to fix it.

Method

Tiffany Lamp

1 Paint the pourer to resemble leadlight. Allow to dry, and varnish.
2 Cut the curler to the required length.
3 Shave the spikes off the side of the curler.
4 Fix the glass bead to the top of the curler to look like a bulb.
5 Mount curler on button base.
6 Place the pourer on the bulb, and top with a collar stud.
7 Attach the tiny bead cap to one end of the twine and the small bead cap to the other.
8 Glue the tiny bead cap to the side of the curler, at its base.
9 Glue the watch winder to the gold bead, and the gold bead to the curler, just below the pourer.
10 Paint stand and shaft.

Materials

Tiffany Lamp
Home perm curler
Round glass bead
Fancy button
Clear plastic saltcellar pourer
Collar stud
Tiny bead cap
Small bead cap
Twine or SYLKO
Watch winder
Small gold bead

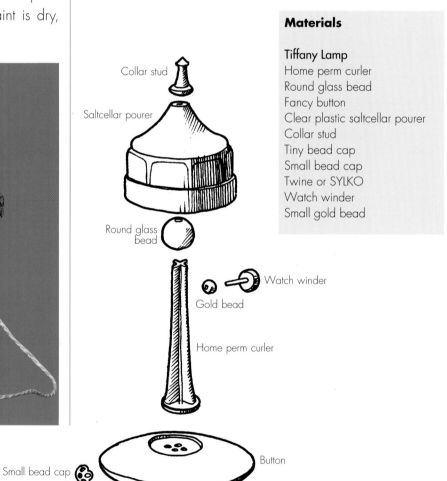

Collar stud
Saltcellar pourer
Round glass bead
Watch winder
Gold bead
Home perm curler
Small bead cap
Button
Twine
Large bead cap

Method

Flower Lamp

1 Bend two short pieces of wire as shown.
2 Glue the glass bead into a bead cap, and thread this onto one of the lengths of wire.
3 Stick the light holder to the other bead cap and attach it to the second length of wire.
4 Pile up, in this order, the curved button, flat button, eyelet and wires.
5 Sandwich the small bead between the tiny rings, and attach this to the length of chain.
6 Fix the chain, with another small bead, to the light holder.
7 Make a cord and plug with twine and bead caps.

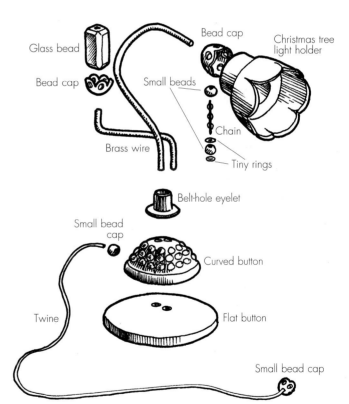

Materials

Flower Lamp
Brass wire
Long glass bead
Large bead caps x 2
Christmas tree light holder
Flat button
Curved button
Belt-hole eyelet
Chain, short length
Small round beads x 2
Tiny rings x 2 (e.g. as found between necklace beads)
Small bead caps x 2
Twine or string

Art Nouveau grandfather clock

Art Nouveau may have been a bit self-conscious, but its creators certainly tried new ways to make old favourites. To emulate it, so did I.

Materials

Card, firm
Clear thick plastic
Watch face
Balsa
Silver foil
Sewing needle
Metal drop earring
Card, light
Plastic curtain hooks x 2
Metal curtain ring
Jewellery, assorted pieces

Method

1 From the firm card, cut the shapes illustrated for the front and back panels.
2 Cut another cabinet shape from the plastic.
3 Trace around the watch face onto the front panel, where the clock face is to be, and cut this circle out.
4 Draw a long oval shape on the front panel where the pendulum is to be, and cut this out.
5 Cut the balsa to the same shape as the clock cabinet.
6 Place the front panel onto the shaped balsa block and trace the holes for the clock face and pendulum onto the balsa.
7 Cut these shapes out.
8 Sink the watch face into the balsa and glue it into position.
9 Line the pendulum hole in the balsa with the silver foil.
10 Glue the end of the needle to the drop earring to make a pendulum.

11 Sink the other end of the needle into the balsa, so that the pendulum is suspended.

12 Line the front panel with the plastic panel, glue them together and trim to fit.

13 Glue the separate layers of the clock cabinet together.

14 Cut a strip from the light card to the width of the cabinet sides and face the raw edges of the balsa with this, sides and top.

15 Attach the curtain hooks to the sides of the clock cabinet.

16 Mask the clock face with paper for protection, then spray paint the clock brown.

17 Frame the clock face with the curtain ring.

18 Decorate the front and top of the cabinet with the odd bits of jewellery, gluing them in place.

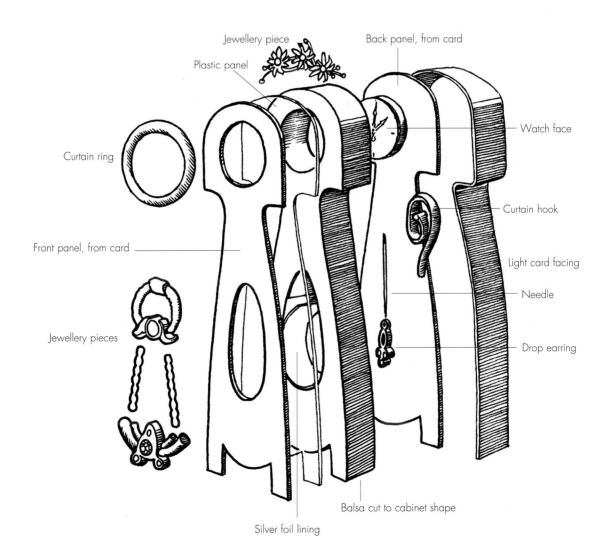

Jewellery piece

Plastic panel

Back panel, from card

Watch face

Curtain ring

Curtain hook

Front panel, from card

Light card facing

Needle

Jewellery pieces

Drop earring

Balsa cut to cabinet shape

Silver foil lining

Art Nouveau tallboy

This piece looks fiddly, but don't despair! The framework is made from card and the elaborate decoration from various jewellery findings.

Materials
Card, heavy
Card, light
Small rectangular bracelet links
Eyes from hook and eye fasteners
Jewellery piece, preferably with
    holes that can be seen through
Brooch
Drop earring
Plastic curtain hooks
Brass tack

Method
1 Cut the back and sides (*see* p55) from the heavy card in one piece. Score and bend.
2 Cut the shelf baffle, drawer and cupboard pieces from the heavy card. Score and bend.
3 Glue the bottom shelf in place.
4 Glue the shaped baffle below the bottom shelf, at the front.
5 Fix the upright cupboard in the centre of the frame, and glue it to the bottom shelf.
6 Glue the semicircular shelves either side of this cupboard.
7 Bend the main sides of the tallboy around and glue the drawer unit in place, resting on the upright cupboard.
8 Cut false drawer panels from the light card and stick these to the front of the drawer unit.
9 Glue the bracelet links to the centre of these panels.

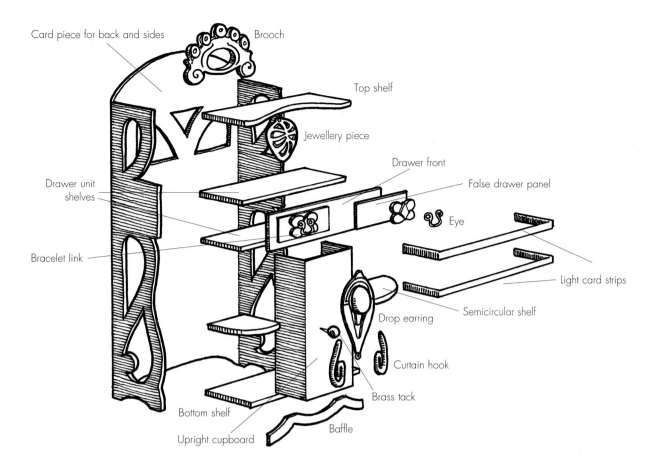

Card piece for back and sides

Brooch

Top shelf

Jewellery piece

Drawer front

False drawer panel

Drawer unit shelves

Eye

Bracelet link

Light card strips

Semicircular shelf

Drop earring

Curtain hook

Brass tack

Bottom shelf

Baffle

Upright cupboard

10 Use the eyes from the fasteners in the centre of the bracelet links to form drawer pulls.

11 Trim with a thin strip of light card across the top and the bottom of this drawer unit. Cut separate strips for the front and sides, or wrap a continuous length around.

12 Glue a jewellery piece over the hole in the centre back of the sideboard.

13 Stick the top shelf in place.

14 Top the whole tallboy with the brooch.

15 Decorate the front of the upright cupboard with the drop earring and curtain hooks.

16 Fix the brass tack in place on the cupboard front as a handle.

17 Spray paint brown.

Bottles
To make the bottles, use glass beads with interesting shapes, and glue bead caps to them for lids and bases.

Vases
The turquoise vases here are larger beads, topped with a belt-hole eyelet and a sequin, spray painted.

Frames
For the photo frames, remove the stones from earrings and put tiny photos in their place. Photos can be reduced on a photocopier. Using the people in the background of the photo will help with size.

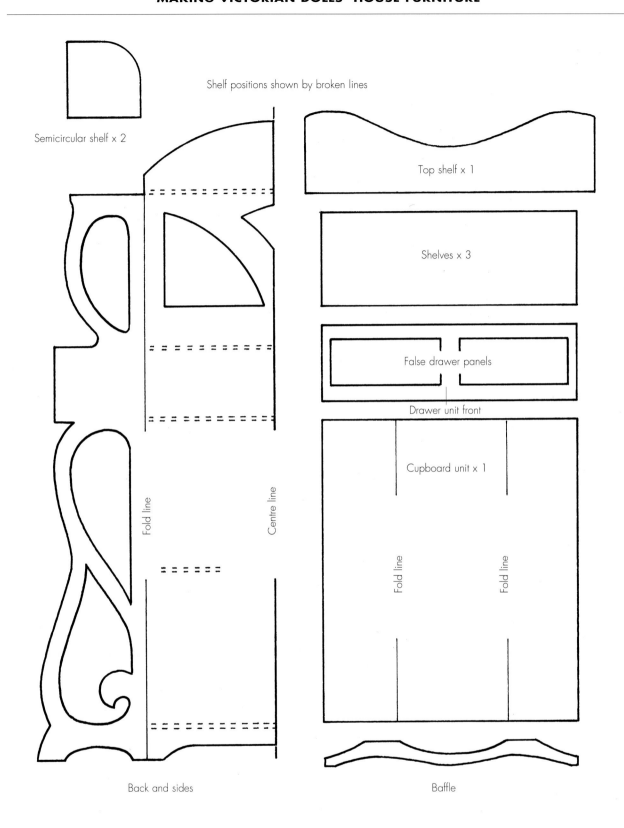

Semicircular shelf x 2

Shelf positions shown by broken lines

Top shelf x 1

Shelves x 3

False drawer panels

Drawer unit front

Cupboard unit x 1

Fold line

Centre line

Fold line

Fold line

Back and sides

Baffle

Art Nouveau screen

The decorative panels on this screen are not as difficult as they appear. Use fancy bracelet links, cutting away the card from the screen to fit them in.

Materials
Card, heavy
Leaf brooch
Large plastic curtain ring, cut in half
Fancy bracelet links x 6
Large bead caps x 5
Small bead caps x 3
Card, light

Method
1 Cut a rectangle of the heavy card to the size of the screen.
2 Turn the screen over and score two lines, one-third of the way in from each side. Bend the card along these lines to form the three panels.
3 Place the brooch at the top of the middle panel and trace around it. Remove the brooch.
4 Place the half curtain rings at the tops of the side panels and trace around them. Remove the rings.
5 Cut the screen top to the shape you have drawn.
6 Glue the brooch and half rings in place to finish off the top edge.
7 Place the bracelet links where you want the decoration to be, and trace around them.

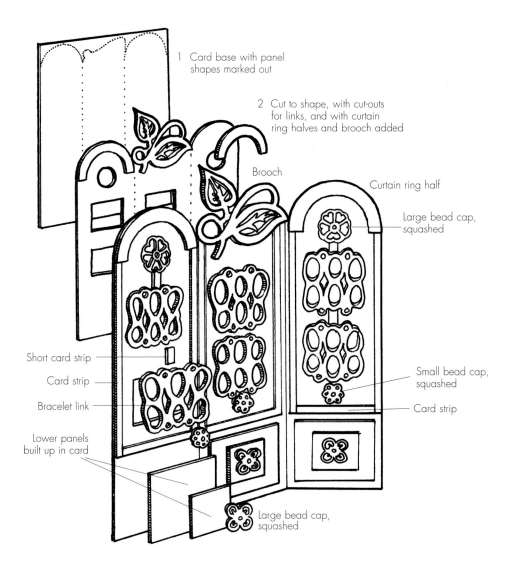

1 Card base with panel shapes marked out

2 Cut to shape, with cut-outs for links, and with curtain ring halves and brooch added

Brooch

Curtain ring half

Large bead cap, squashed

Short card strip

Card strip

Bracelet link

Small bead cap, squashed

Card strip

Lower panels built up in card

Large bead cap, squashed

8 Cut out the card, just inside your pencil line, so that the holes are smaller than the links. If a simple rectangular hole doesn't interfere with your link's pattern, cut out an appropriate size rectangle instead.

9 Glue the links over the front of the holes.

10 Place one large bead cap, squashed, at the top of each side panel, and trace around it. Cut out the holes slightly smaller again, so that the bead caps fit over them.

11 Fix one small bead cap, squashed, below the bottom link on each panel.

12 Decorate the lower part of each panel with successive squares of the light card, each one smaller than the last.

13 Decorate the centre of these panels with squashed bead caps.

14 Cut strips of card to form a frame around the sides and base of each upper panel, and glue into place.

15 Cut short strips of card to trim the side panels, between the bracelet links and large bead caps.

16 Spray paint gold.

Art Nouveau sideboard

This whole piece of furniture came about when I found a handbag clasp that looked to me like Art Nouveau: everything else was tailored to this.

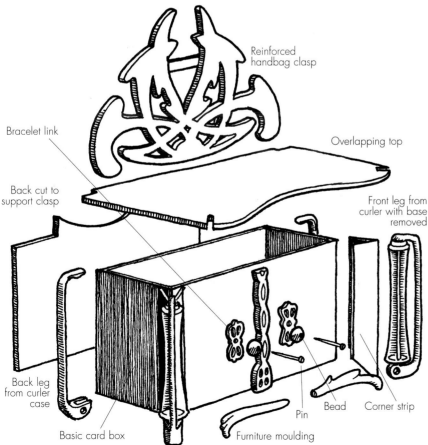

Reinforced handbag clasp

Overlapping top

Bracelet link

Back cut to support clasp

Front leg from curler with base removed

Back leg from curler case

Basic card box

Furniture moulding

Pin

Bead

Corner strip

Materials

Card, heavy
Fancy handbag clasp
Home perm curlers x 2
Stick-on furniture moulding
Jewellery pieces
Small rectangular bracelet links x 2
Pins x 2
Small round beads x 2

Method

1 Cut the back panel and sideboard top from the card.
2 Make up the box in card by scoring and bending.
3 Cut, score and bend strips of card to fit around the corners at either side of the front.
4 Cut a card back for the sideboard which will fit and reinforce the clasp without interfering with the pattern. Trace the pattern of the clasp onto the card and cut this out.
5 Glue the clasp onto the card, and the card to the sideboard top.
6 Attach the sideboard top and the back panel.
7 Place the outer case of a curler at each back corner and glue into place.
8 Add a curler, minus the outer case, to each front corner.
9 Decorate the front of the sideboard with furniture mouldings and jewellery pieces.
10 Glue the bracelet links to the front of the sideboard.
11 Insert the pins through the beads and then through the centre of the bracelet links and into the front of the sideboard.
12 Spray paint brown.

Fork chairs

Forks have long intrigued me (they have such nice shapes!) and when I started on Art Nouveau, I realized they were just the thing for chair backs. The only problem is that the weight of the metal forks tends to make the chairs topple. I suppose you could use plastic ones but the shapes are not so elegant.

Materials
Card, firm
Balsa or heavy card
Cocktail forks x 4 (optional)
Wadding
Fabric
Fork

Method

1   Cut two bases to the width of the fork, one from firm card and the other from balsa.
2   Upholster the card base.
3   Use firm card strips for the legs and stiles.
4   Make indentations in the balsa to take the prongs of the fork. Cut the handle off the fork and fix in position.
5   Insert the upholstered seat.

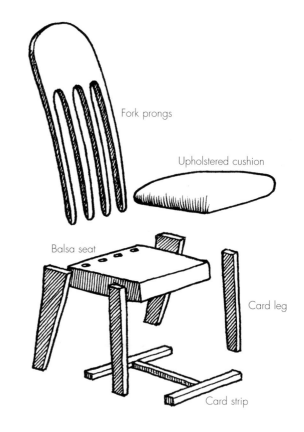

Fork prongs

Upholstered cushion

Balsa seat

Card leg

Card strip

10 Lounge

I wanted the lounge to be warm and richly decorated, so I chose the giftwrap, to be used for wallpaper, accordingly. I used a commercial rug to cover the floor. The mirror is a piece from a takeaway food container, glued in a brooch frame. The lights at the side of the mirror I made by gluing Christmas tree light holders to bead caps that I opened out, and gluing 'crystal' beads inside these. For the grandfather clock in the lounge, I adapted the Art Nouveau grandfather clock (*see* Hummer Peacock Room, p52).

Louis XIV sideboard

To get the distinctive front panel of this sideboard, I used a toilet roll cylinder cut in half. The beads across the front edges aren't individually stuck on! I used ball-and-socket chain cut to size.

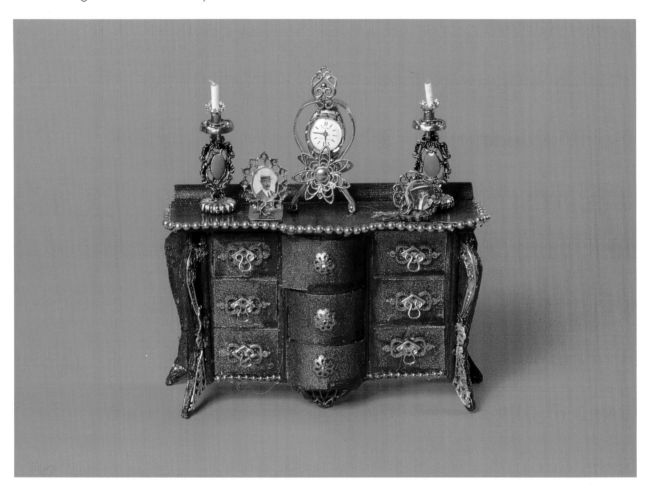

Materials

Card, light
Toilet roll cylinder
Balsa
Wood, thin ply
Quarter-round wood strip
Small beads x 3
Pins x 3
Small rectangular bracelet
  links x 6
Eyes from hook and eye
  fasteners x 6
Fancy bracelet link
Ball-and-socket 'bobble' chain
Fancy jewellery pieces, thin
  enough to cut

Method

1 Make up the box shape out of four light card panels, as shown.
2 Glue the curved corners together to get the distinctive shape of the legs.
3 Cut the toilet roll cylinder in half, vertically.
4 Measure the toilet roll against the front of the sideboard, cut to fit, and glue in place.
5 Reinforce inside the cabinet and the toilet roll with balsa.
6 Cut nine false drawer panels from the card and glue them in place.
7 Cut a top from the wood to the shape of the cabinet, but slightly larger. Glue this in place.
8 Finish the top by running a length of the quarter-round wood strip across the back, and gluing it in place.
9 Spray paint brown.

10 Place the small bead caps in the centre of the curved drawers and secure them with pins, sticking them through the bead caps and toilet roll.

11 Decorate the centre of each of the side drawers with a bracelet link.

12 Glue an eye from a hook and eye fastener to each of the bracelet links.

13 Stick the fancy bracelet link below the toilet roll, for decoration.

14 Run the ball-and-socket chain around the top and along the base of the sideboard, gluing it in place.

15 Cut up the fancy jewellery pieces to fit the cabinet legs and glue them in place. I used half a drop earring for the top curve.

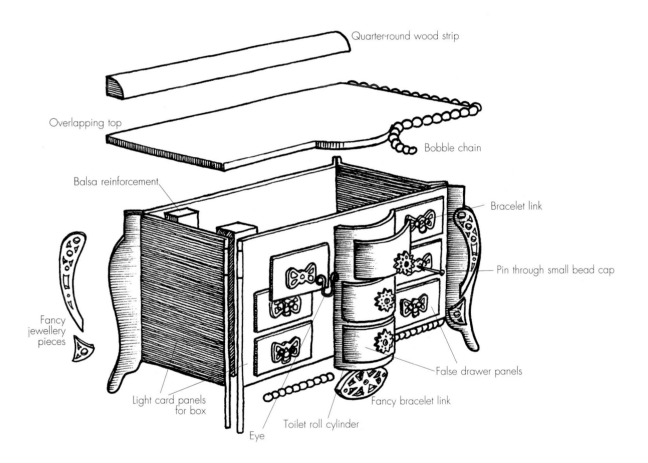

Quarter-round wood strip

Overlapping top

Bobble chain

Balsa reinforcement

Bracelet link

Pin through small bead cap

Fancy jewellery pieces

False drawer panels

Light card panels for box

Fancy bracelet link

Eye

Toilet roll cylinder

Candlesticks

When you make tiny decorations like these, your versions will differ from mine because the 'ingredients' will vary. Using a glue gun as I do helps to stick odd-shaped pieces together as it leaves a pad of glue to act as a bridge between the different shapes. Very useful!

Method

1. Cut a tiny piece out of the button shafts so that they will sit astride the earring drops.
2. For each candlestick glue together, in the following order, the flat button with milled edges, earring drop, flat button, belt-hole eyelet, and bead cap opened out.
3. To make the candles, use Copydex to stick a length of SYLKO across a strip of paper, with the ends of the SYLKO overhanging.
4. Wet the end of the paper and roll it tightly around a needle. Twist the needle backwards to release it.
5. Seal along the width of the paper, and cut it in half to produce two candles.
6. Trim the wicks.
7. Glue the candles to the bead caps.

Paper candle

Bead cap

Eyelet

Flat button

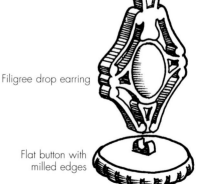

Filigree drop earring

Flat button with milled edges

Materials

Flat buttons with shaft x 2
Filigree drop earrings x 2
Flat buttons with milled edges
 and shafts x 2
Belt-hole eyelets x 2
Filigree bead caps x 2
Paper
White SYLKO

Clock

There are dozens of ways to make clocks. This one is based on a spring clip made to hang gloves onto a handbag strap. They may not be needed for their intended purpose nowadays but they still have a use!

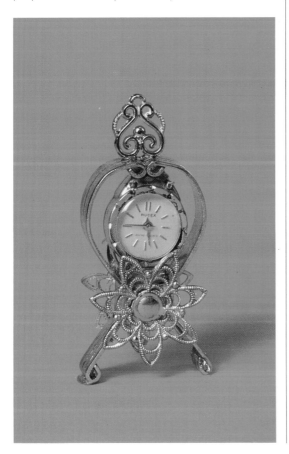

Method

1   Glue the watch in the centre of the clip.
2   Decorate the front of the clip with jewellery pieces.
3   Leave the top plain or, if you like, decorate it with a jewellery finding.

Materials
Old watch face
Glove clip
Jewellery pieces

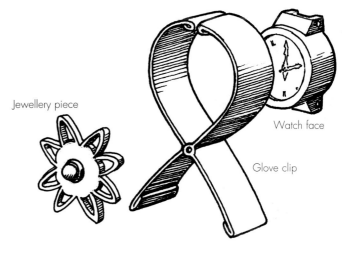

Jewellery piece

Watch face

Glove clip

Queen Anne circular occasional table

For the table top, cut the pattern from a magazine. If trimming your pattern to fit the table will spoil the design, you could try reducing it on a photocopier. Of course, unless you have access to a colour photocopier, you will then have to colour it later. Alternatively, you could paint or draw your own design.

Method

1 Slip the bracelet onto the tin lid to make sure it fits. If it is too large, cut a small piece out and glue the ends together. If it is too small, find another bracelet or lid! It helps to keep the bracelet on the lid while you are making the table, but do not glue it in place yet, as you will have to remove it later to spray paint the legs and lower part.
2 Place the picture on the lid to make sure that it fits inside the bracelet frame. Trim it to fit .
3 Mount the fitted picture on a circle of card, and put aside.
4 Remove the curlers from their clips and use the clips for legs. (Don't throw the curlers away! They make very good legs of another type.)
5 Cut the legs to the length you desire.
6 Put the curlers into boiling water until they are soft enough to curl the ends for feet. Using pliers for this will make the job easier.
7 File the tops of the curler clips flat.
8 Cut four half circles of balsa to replace the balls of the curlers. The balsa circles should have the same diameter as the curler balls.
9 Glue the half circles to the table, flat end down.
10 Attach each leg top astride a balsa half circle.
11 Remove the bracelet and spray paint the rest of the table dark brown.
12 When the paint is dry, glue the picture onto the tin top and frame it with the bracelet.
13 Decorate the tops of the legs with the pieces of gold jewellery.
14 Cut the bead cap into quarters and use a quarter to decorate each foot.
15 Glue the chain links to the side of the table, one between each pair of legs.

Materials
Gold- coloured metal bracelet
Tin lid ½in (12mm) deep
Circular picture
Card, firm
Home perm curlers x 4
Balsa
Gold jewellery pieces
Gold bead cap
Gold chain links x 4

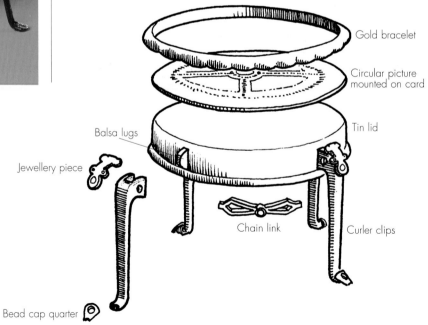

Gold bracelet

Circular picture mounted on card

Tin lid

Balsa lugs

Jewellery piece

Chain link

Curler clips

Bead cap quarter

Newspaper rack

If you want curved legs for the newspaper rack, use an oval buckle to make them. For straight legs, use a square or rectangular one.

Method

1 Remove the centre strut from the buckle.
2 Cut the buckle in half to make the legs.
3 Cut a length of balsa, equal to the width you want the newspaper rack to be.
4 Stick the buckle halves either side of the balsa so that they stand firm.
5 Cut a rectangle from the card, with the width slightly longer than the width of the newspaper rack, and the length to that of the balsa.
6 Glue the card to the top of the balsa.
7 Attach the belt links to the sides of the card, scoring and bending the card to make sides just high enough to hold the belt links firm. The links should be angled out slightly.
8 Spray paint.

Materials

Fancy buckle
Balsa
Card, heavy
Rectangular filigree metal belt links x 2

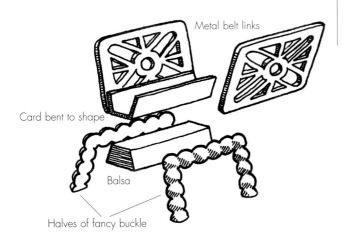

Metal belt links

Card bent to shape

Balsa

Halves of fancy buckle

Scent-bottle top

Brooch

Button

Chignon pins

Button shelf

Fern stand

This is one of the easiest things to make in the book, so if you want something easy to start on, I recommend this.

Method

1 Turn the brooch upside down and glue a small button under it.
2 Glue the tops of each pin to the underside of the brooch so that the button reinforces them.
3 Wedge the other button between the legs, halfway down, to form a shelf.
4 Spray paint.

Materials
Circular brooch
Small buttons x 2
Chignon pins x 4

Potted Ferns
Ferns were so much a part of the Victorian drawing room, it seemed important to find a way to represent them. I had some success with cutting and rolling a Harrods' bag (just the right shade of green), but it was when I became the proud owner of a tatty feather duster that I knew I had the answer! I cut the feathers off the duster, stuck them individually in a chunk of oasis, and sprayed them with green cellulose paint. Not only did this colour the feathers, it stiffened them as well, allowing me to cut, bend and shape them.

Pots
Scent bottles and their tops both make handy pots, and a clip earring opened up makes a good plant shelf.

Sofa

For modelling, if you can forget the function of objects and just look at their shapes, you will find some very interesting materials. When the curve of this pair of sunglasses caught my eye, I saw immediately what I wanted them to be – a sofa back!

Method

1 Remove the arms from the sunglasses.
2 Cut four shapes from the card, and four from the wadding, to fit both sides of the lenses.
3 Cut four pieces of velvet to the shape of the lenses, but so that they overhang all around.
4 For each piece, lay the wadding on the reverse side of the velvet. Do not glue it yet: wadding and glue don't mix.
5 Make little cuts in the velvet, towards the card, all around.
6 Place the card upside down on the wadding and velvet, then fold and glue the little strips of velvet down.
7 Trim any spare velvet.
8 Glue upholstered cushions to the backs and fronts of the lenses.
9 Cut a base from the balsa to fit the top curves of the sunglasses' frame.
10 Trace the outline of the balsa base onto the card and cut this out.
11 Upholster the card base, following the instructions above.
12 Cut the three furniture decorations in half.
13 Cut balsa pieces to fit four of the decoration halves, and reinforce the decorations with these.
14 Mount the four halves onto the balsa base as legs.
15 Fill in the nose arch with the drop earring.
16 Glue the glasses to the back of the balsa base.
17 Fit the remaining two furniture halves to the sides of the glasses, as arms. Do not glue them to the base, as the upholstered seat will be inserted later.
18 Spray paint.
19 Insert the upholstered seat, glue it to the base, and glue the arms to the seat.
20 Decorate the front and sides of the seat base with the lampshade gimp.

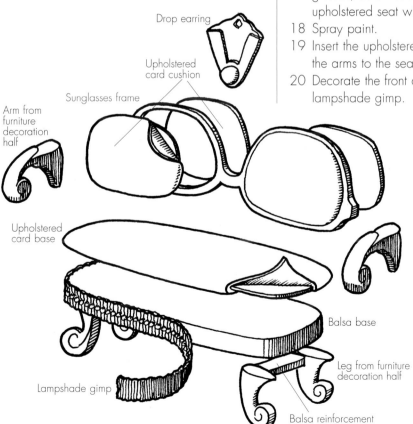

Drop earring

Upholstered card cushion

Sunglasses frame

Arm from furniture decoration half

Upholstered card base

Lampshade gimp

Balsa base

Leg from furniture decoration half

Balsa reinforcement

Materials

Sunglasses
Card, medium
Wadding
Old velvet (new velvet is too inflexible)
Balsa
Stick-on furniture decorations x 3
Drop earring
Lampshade gimp

Chess table

Draw the squares for the chessboard onto plain paper, but if you are lucky enough to find checked paper you can use, do so!

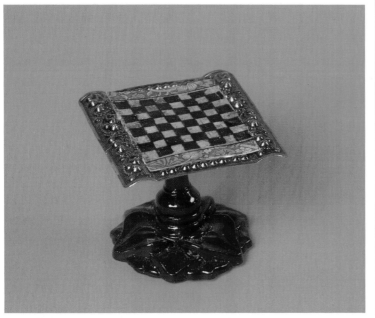

Method

1   Remove any stones from the brooch, cut the top off the pawn, and glue the pawn to the centre of the brooch or button.
2   Draw around the hole in the button, and cut a piece of firm card to slightly overlap it. This will form the table top.
3   Back the buckle with card.
4   Glue the reinforced buckle to the top of the chesspiece.
5   Spray paint brown.
6   Cut paper to fit the card table top, and draw the chessboard on it. Mount this on the brooch, and fill in any spaces with giftwrap.
7   Glue the table top to the button, and the button to the chesspiece.
8   Finish with a couple of coats of varnish.

Materials
Chesspiece, pawn
Fancy button or brooch
Rectangular buckle
Card, firm
Plain paper
Decorative giftwrap
Flat button

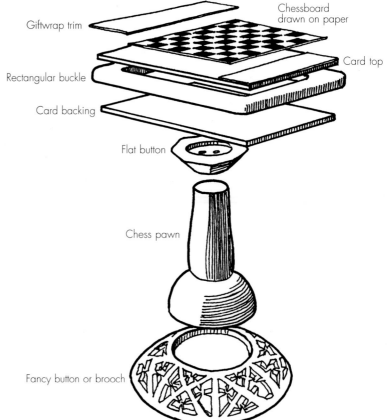

Giftwrap trim

Chessboard drawn on paper

Card top

Rectangular buckle

Card backing

Flat button

Chess pawn

Fancy button or brooch

11 Bathroom

I was so charmed with the stained glass in the hall I decided, when it came to making the bathroom, to have stained glass panels in a frieze all around the tops of the walls. As with the hall I made a pull-out box through which the light could shine, but this time I used stiff, clear plastic from a chocolate box cover and traced the designs from a source book using a fine, black overhead projector pen. I then filled the design in with colour and it looked very authentic. Dolls' house tile papers are very good but tend to come in small sheets so I only used them for the floor and for strips to trim the walls. The square-patterned wallpaper is from a child's arithmetic book.

Mahogany-encased bath

You will need to look closely at bubble packs to find your basic bath shape. Clear bubble packs over padlocks with keys, over sweeteners and over drawer handles can provide good bath shapes.

Materials
Clear plastic bubble pack
Card, firm
Marbled paper or Fablon
Dark woodgrain paper
Illustrations of tiles
Card, thin

Method
1 Cut the plastic carefully away from the backing card, leaving a border of plastic or card.
2 Trace around the top of the bubble pack onto the firm card, and cut this out to give a frame a little larger than the 'bath'.
3 Cut out the shape of the bath from the centre of this frame.
4 Cover the frame with marbled paper or Fablon.
5 Spray paint the bubble pack, and leave to dry.
6 Glue the frame to the bath.
7 Make up a box from firm card to fit the bubble pack and frame.
8 Score and bend a piece of firm card to make the end and side splashback for the bath. Cover with woodgrain paper and glue a strip of tiles across it, as shown above. Glue to the top of the bath.

9 Cut two narrow strips of firm card to run across the top of the
   splashback, mitre one end of each to form a neat corner, cover
   with woodgrain paper, and glue in place.
10 Cover the sheet of thin card with woodgrain paper, and cut strips
   from this for panelling.
11 Glue tiles onto side and end of bath, as shown above, then
   panel around them with the strips of covered card.
12 Glue a large strip of covered card to the end of the bath and glue
   strips for panels on this.
13 Cut narrow strips of card to neaten the top of the bath. Cover with
   woodgrain paper, and glue in place.
14 Paint all cut edges of panelling brown. (I used watercolour for this.)

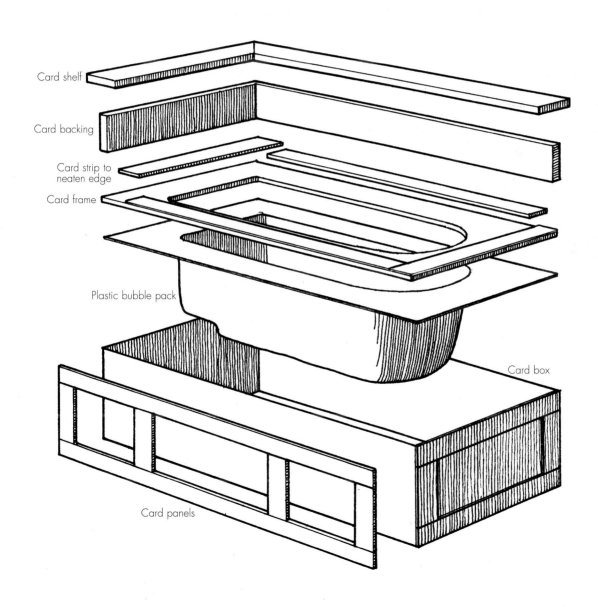

Card shelf

Card backing

Card strip to
neaten edge

Card frame

Plastic bubble pack

Card box

Card panels

Mixer taps

I quite terrified myself making these, but I've done it and they look okay, if you don't look too closely! Now I'm terrified of trying to show you how to make them. Fortunately they are much in fashion, so you should be able to find a photo in a catalogue to refer to.

Materials
Cuff link
Screw-type necklace fasteners x 2
Solid necklace link
Small gold beads x 2
Pins x 2
Small gold bead caps x 2
Belt-hole eyelet
Fine wire
Small screw-type necklace fastener
Small beads x 2
Tiny hollow cylinder
Larger bead
Tiny gold bell
Rolled chain
Necklace hook

Method

1 Cut the top off the cuff link. This top part will not be used.
2 Only the screw halves of the necklace fasteners are used. Stick these, screws pointing forward, over the holes on either side of the solid necklace link. You may need to cut the link from the back of the fastener.
3 Glue the small gold beads behind them.
4 Stick a pin through each bead cap and insert these pins into the screw holes of the necklace fasteners. This forms the taps.
5 Glue the necklace link behind the 'legs' of the cufflink.
6 Glue the eyelet to the top of the legs.
7 Onto a piece of fine wire thread in turn, the small necklace fastener, small bead, cylinder, small bead, larger bead, and bell.

8 Fix all of these in place.

9 Bend the bell over to form the shower nozzle.

10 Attach one end of the chain to the small fastener on the shower head assembly, trimming the wire if necessary, and glue the other end to the eyelet on the tap assembly.

11 Bend the necklace hook and insert it, at an angle, between the legs of the cuff link. This forms the on/off lever.

12 To install the mixer taps in the bath, glue the bottom of the cuff link bar to the top of the bath.

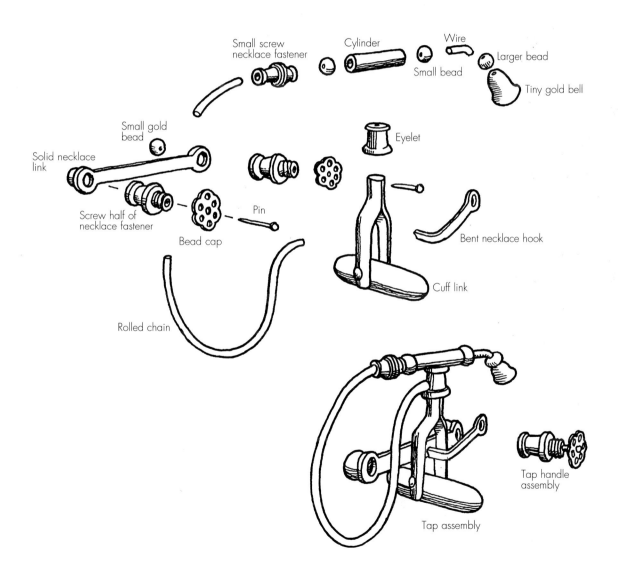

Small screw necklace fastener

Cylinder

Wire

Larger bead

Small bead

Tiny gold bell

Small gold bead

Eyelet

Solid necklace link

Screw half of necklace fastener

Pin

Bent necklace hook

Bead cap

Cuff link

Rolled chain

Tap handle assembly

Tap assembly

Built-in corner washstand

Cut a small piece from the end of an eraser for soap, and use a glass button for a soap dish.

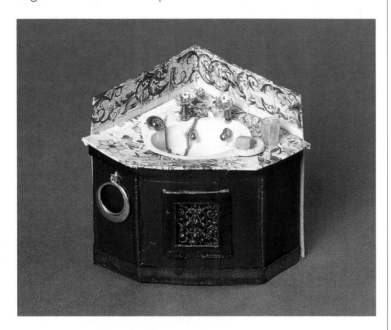

Card splashback

Jam container

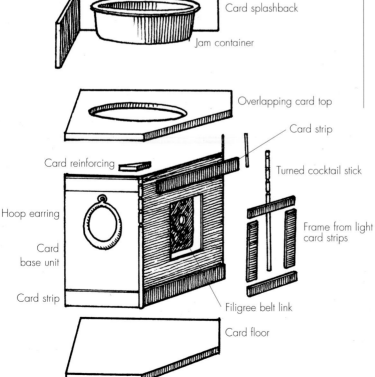

Overlapping card top

Card strip

Card reinforcing

Turned cocktail stick

Hoop earring

Frame from light card strips

Card base unit

Card strip

Filigree belt link

Card floor

Method

1 Cut the medium card for the base unit, as shown in the drawing.
2 Score and bend to form sides.
3 Place the link in the centre front of the unit and trace around it.
4 Cut a hole slightly smaller than this outline.
5 Glue the link behind the hole.
6 Frame the link with strips of light card to neaten it.
7 Bend the unit into shape and glue it together, reinforcing the corners with more card if necessary.
8 Place the unit on the medium card, trace around it and cut the piece out. This will form the floor of the washbasin.
9 Cut a second piece out to the same shape, but extend the sides and front a little to make the top, which will slightly overlap the unit.
10 Place the jam container in the centre of the unit top and trace around its base.
11 Cut this shape out to take the jam container.
12 Cover the washstand's top with the giftwrap.
13 Glue the jam container into the unit top.
14 Attach the floor of the washbasin.
15 Pin or glue the hoop earring to the top of one of the side panels.
16 Cut a splashback from the light card to fit across the back of the unit.
17 Cover the splashback with giftwrap and stick it to the unit

Materials
Card, medium
Rectangular filigree belt link
Card, light
Plastic jam container, single portion
Giftwrap
Pin
Hoop earring

Flusher WC

You will be flushed with success when you make this WC!

Materials

Roll-on deodorant bottle, plastic
Balsa
Card, firm
Bugle beads x 2
Giftwrap
Single serve butter containers x 2
Jump rings x 2
Small round bead or solid
  chain link
Chain
Long solid chain link
Drinking straw
Hair dye tube nozzle
Stabilo boss highlighter lid
Foamcore
Textured paper (optional)
Tile illustrations
Three-into-one necklace fasteners
  x 3 (1 optional)
Shiny cardboard (e.g.
  takeaway lid)
Tissue paper
Thin wire

Method

1 Cut across the top of the deodorant bottle, about 1 in (25.5mm) below the neck. If you place an elastic band around the bottle, it will give you a line to cut on.
2 Remove the roll-on ball from the bottle. Turn the bottle upside down and you have the toilet bowl.
3 For the lower lid, cut a half oval shape from the balsa, to fit over the hole of the toilet base.
4 For the upper lid cut an oval from the card, and this time cut a groove across the back of the oval, where the hinges will go. Insert two bugle beads in the groove. They shine and will look like hinges.
5 Stick the upper and lower lids together. Glue the toilet lid to the toilet bowl.
6 Decorate the toilet bowl with selected patterns from giftwrap. Varnish.
7 Glue two single-serve butter containers together, edge to edge, for the cistern.
8 Trim the back ridge off the containers so that the cistern will sit flat against the wall.
9 Decorate the cistern with giftwrap patterns. Varnish.
10 Using the jump rings, attach the small bead or chain link to one end of the chain, and the long link to the other.

11 Bore a hole in the side of the cistern, above the central flange, and insert the free end of the link into this. If you don't have a suitable link, insert a piece of wire into the cistern and bend the other end into a hook to hold the chain. Disguise the join with a jewellery piece.

12 Use the drinking straw for the downpipe, and cut to the length required.

13 Fix the downpipe in the dye tube nozzle at one end, and in the high-lighter lid at the other.

14 Join the three sections of the toilet together, gluing the highlighter lid to the toilet lid, and the hair dye nozzle to the cistern.

15 Cut a piece of Foamcore for the wall behind the toilet, and cover with textured paper and/or tile illustrations, to suit your bathroom.

16 Glue the toilet to the wall.

17 Cut one of the necklace fasteners in half, and use these halves for hinges, to decorate each side of the toilet bowl, where it joins the wall. You may also like to attach hinges to the side of the cistern, at its base.

18 Cut a small strip of shiny cardboard. Bend this around the downpipe, a little way above the highlighter lid, and glue the ends to the wall.

**Toilet Roll and Holder
To make a toilet roll, wrap some tissue paper around a straw, and cut to size. For the holder, mount a three-into-one necklace clasp on a small piece of balsa, and cut the balsa to shape. Wire the toilet roll to the balsa.**

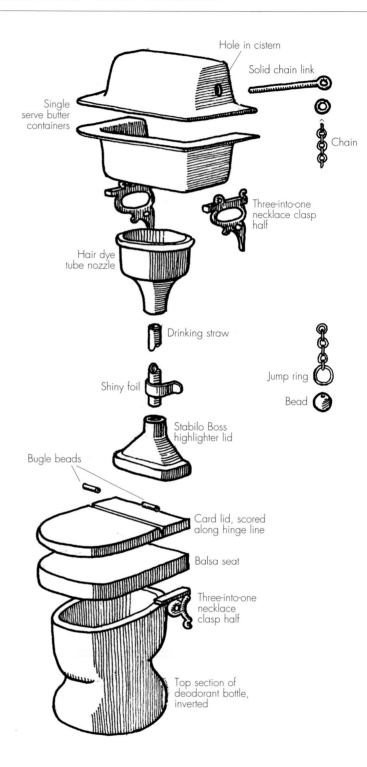

Hole in cistern

Solid chain link

Chain

Single serve butter containers

Three-into-one necklace clasp half

Hair dye tube nozzle

Drinking straw

Jump ring

Shiny foil

Bead

Stabilo Boss highlighter lid

Bugle beads

Card lid, scored along hinge line

Balsa seat

Three-into-one necklace clasp half

Top section of deodorant bottle, inverted

Radiator

The main 'ingredient' for this is Acco fasteners. These come in two parts, male and female. The male part has fold-over lugs at the top and bottom.

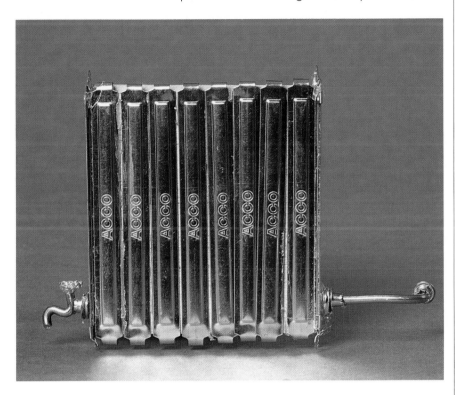

Materials
Card, firm
Clips x 8
Brass wire
Small bead cap
Belt-hole eyelets x 3

Method

1 Cut a piece of card to fit the eight clips.
2 Drape the clips over the card, bending the lugs over at the top and bottom and gluing them in place as you go.
3 Glue a female clip to both ends to disguise the raw ends of the card.
4 Bend the wire to the shape of a tap.
5 Stick the small bead cap to this to form the handle.
6 Glue the tap to the belt hole eyelet.
7 Fix the belt-hole eyelet to one side of the radiator, at the bottom.
8 Thread and glue the other two belt-hole eyelets onto a short length of wire to make the lead-in pipe.
9 Glue one eyelet to the radiator and the other to the wall.

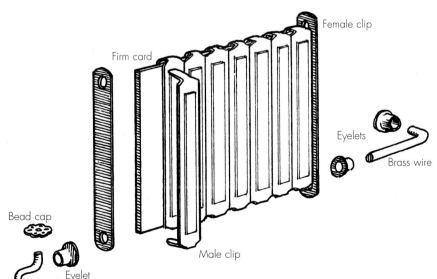

Firm card

Female clip

Eyelets

Brass wire

Bead cap

Brass wire

Eyelet

Male clip

Gold oil heater

Although this heater looks elaborate, it is really hardly more than a small box decorated with bracelet links!

Materials

35mm film box
Large rectangular metal bracelet
  links x 2
Small rectangular metal bracelet
  links x 2
Card, firm
Large square metal bracelet link
Small square metal bracelet link
Dress stud
Three-into-one necklace clasp
Trouser waistband fastener
Embossed foil strip (e.g. for
  cake decoration)
Stick-on furniture curlicues x 2
Curtain ring
Long, solid necklace links x 2
Small round beads x 2

Method

1 Arrange your links on the box. (I used a large one either side and two small ones in front.)
2 Make a card lid to overlap the top. Back the large link with card, and glue this to the lid.
3 Back the small link with card, and glue this to the large link. Top the lot with a dress stud.
4 Use a necklace clasp as a shelf halfway up the front panel.
5 Glue a wasteband fastener at the bottom of the front panel for a second shelf.
6 Bind all around the bottom of the stove, using embossed foil strip.
7 Place strips of card above each side panel.
8 Glue on one curlicue front and back, for legs.
9 Cut the curtain ring in half and attach one half to each side for handles.
10 Spray paint gold.
11 Stick a long link at one side of each door for hinges, and glue the beads to the doors for handles.

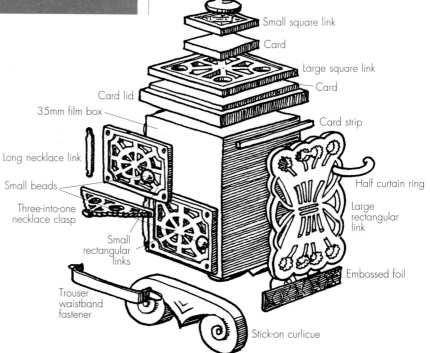

Dress stud
Small square link
Card
Large square link
Card
Card lid
Card strip
35mm film box
Long necklace link
Half curtain ring
Small beads
Large rectangular link
Three-into-one necklace clasp
Small rectangular links
Embossed foil
Trouser waistband fastener
Stick-on curlicue

Wrought iron towel stand

This is very easy to make, provided you can find the right kind of fan!

Materials
Plastic filigree fan
Small rectangular bracelet link
Large rectangular bracelet link

Method
1 Cut two identical lengths of fan to form the sides.
2 Trim the pattern of the sides to the shape you like.
3 Glue the small link between the sides to form a shelf, which will also reinforce them.
4 Glue the large link to the top.
5 Spray paint white.

Large link

Small link

Section of plastic fan

12 Alleyway and Scullery

I'd had the idea of an alleyway and scullery in mind for a while, full of beer crates, an old sink, a copper and the sort of junk that accumulates in such places, but it only began to take shape when I happened on a plastic video cassette rack in a jumble sale! I realized it would make a perfect alleyway roof, but I needed a second one to complete the length I wanted. I scoured local boot sales, but it was ages before I found anything that would do. What I did eventually find was an audio cassette rack, so it was smaller than the first, but that's half the fun in this game! What you find so often dictates the results you get.

I turned the two cassettes upside down and used them as roofs, making the alleyway buildings to fit. The windows were made from a commercial one cut carefully across the middle, and the ladder from a piece of commercial railing cut down. The walls were easy to decorate. I simply covered them with brick paper. The copper I built in last.

Sink and draining board

Here is the one time you want dirty dishes and clutter, so make the most of it!

Method

1 Cut three pillars from the balsa, to the height that you want your sink and draining board, with one pillar slightly longer than the others, so that the draining board sits at an angle.
2 Cover the pillars with brick paper.
3 Cut a draining board from the balsa and score runnels in it. Use the razor blade box for your sink.
4 Space the pillars to support the sink and draining board and glue them into position.
5 Glue the sink and draining board onto the pillars.
6 Use white buttons for plates, or commercial dolls' house plates.
7 Cut the tops off the medicine capsules to form cups and use half chain links glued to the side if you want handles.
8 Pile the plates and cups higgledy-piggledy in the sink and on the draining board.
9 Cut shelves from the balsa to fit under the sink, and glue them into place.
10 Stick the pin into one of the pillars and hang a towel on this.

**Towels and Washing
I used textured paper for all cloth, including washing, as it hangs better. Cut it to size and draw on lines and patterns with felt pens.**

Balsa draining board, scored

Watch winder

Pin

Wire

Five-pack razor blade box

Balsa shelf

Balsa pillar

Materials
Balsa
Brick paper
Five-pack razor blade box
White buttons or dolls' house plates
Medicine capsules
Circular chain links
Pin

Copper

Use brick paper to cover this copper, which is simple, but effective.

Method

1 Cut out the shape as shown from the firm card.
2 Score along the dotted lines and bend the card into shape.
3 Cover the card with brick paper.
4 Cut out a door in the front panel.
5 Make a card frame for the door, as shown, from light card.
6 Glue the bead to one side of the door for a handle.
7 Spray paint the door black.
8 Cut a top for the copper from the firm card or from featherboard.
9 Spray paint the top white and when the paint has dried, glue it in place.
10 Cut a circle of balsa for a lid and score at intervals to resemble planks.
11 Cut a handle from the balsa and glue this to the lid.
12 Cut a floor from the light card, the same shape as the top, and glue it in place.
13 Glue the copper into a corner of the wall.
14 Cut small balsa strips and run them along the back of the copper to seal where the brick meets the wall.
15 Glue the jewellery piece or clasp to the top of the door for decoration.
16 You may want to stick a pin in the top of the copper to hang a towel or tongs on.

Materials
Card, firm
Brick paper
Card, light
Small bead
Balsa
Jewellery piece or small handbag clasp

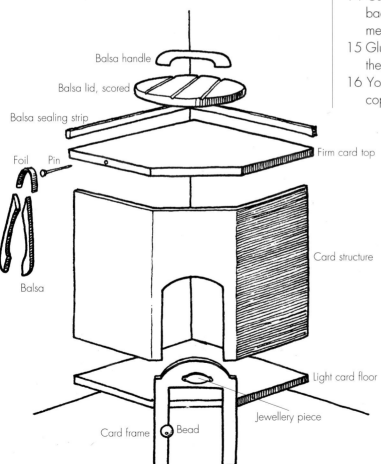

Balsa handle

Balsa lid, scored

Balsa sealing strip

Foil   Pin

Firm card top

Balsa

Card structure

Light card floor

Jewellery piece

Card frame   Bead

Buckets
Use the lids from whisky bottles for buckets. Bend a length of brass wire for the handle, punch holes in the sides of the lid and insert the wire through these.

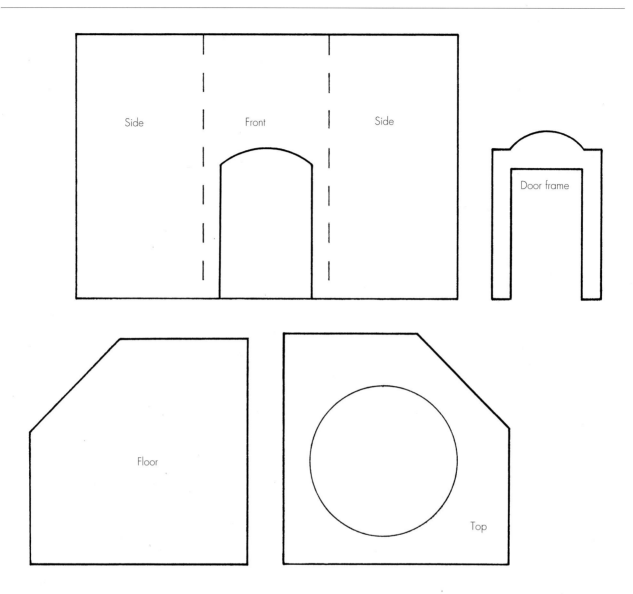

Side

Front

Side

Door frame

Floor

Top

Tongs
Tongs are easy to make and require only balsa and foil (e.g. from a patty tin). Cut two pieces of balsa to the shape shown and attach one to the other by gluing the foil in place.

Dowel handle

Tea stirrer end

Toothbrush

Balsa broom head

Brooms
A broom can be made from a cut of balsa with a length of rod added for a handle. Cover the bottom of the balsa with glue and stick a toothbrush to it by the bristles. When it is firmly stuck, cut away the rest of the toothbrush.

A dustpan broom can be made in the same way, using a tea stirrer in place of the balsa and handle.

Washing machine

I'm afraid I can't tell you what brand of shampoo this plastic lid came from. Someone gave it to me and it reminded me of a Victorian washing machine I'd seen, so that's what it became. Just in case you find one . .

Materials
Card, medium
Shampoo bottle lid
Drinking straw
Card, firm
Small beads x 2
Small bead caps x 3
Brass wire
Small oval bead
Small wheels x 2
Unusually long chain link
Turned cocktail stick
Tea stirrers x 4
Press studs x 4
Picket fencing, gauge 000

Method

1 Make a card top for the open end of the shampoo lid.
2 Cut two lengths from the straw, and glue one on top of the other to make mangle rollers.
3 Frame the rollers with card strip sides and a wooden shelf.
4 Insert another strip of card above the rollers, with its wide face showing.
5 Top the wooden shelf with two bead caps mounted on beads.
6 On one side of the mangle unit, glue the third bead cap to take the handle.
7 Bend the brass wire to shape for the handle, fix the oval bead onto one end, and insert the other end into the bead cap.
8 Glue the two wheels to the lid, with one overlapping the other.
9 Take the long link from the wheels to the lid, at an angle, and fix the cocktail stick to the lid where they join.
10 Use the tea stirrers as legs, setting them at an angle from the centre of the lid.
11 Place a press stud at the end of each leg, for wheels.

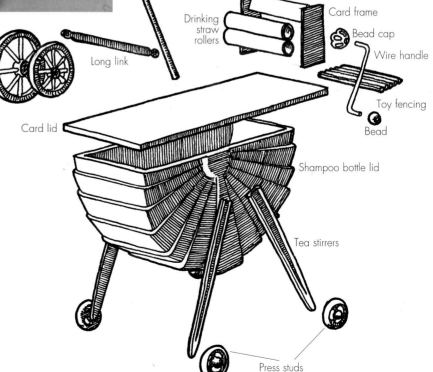

Cocktail stick
Card shelf
Bead caps
Small bead
Drinking straw rollers
Card frame
Bead cap
Wire handle
Toy fencing
Wheels
Long link
Bead
Card lid
Shampoo bottle lid
Tea stirrers
Press studs

Coal hod

If you can find a cigar tube, this is easy.

Method

1 Using scissors, cut the top of the tube to the shape shown.
2 Insert something into the tube to bore against, and punch holes in its sides to take the handle.
3 Bend the brass wire to shape and insert the ends through the bead caps and into the holes in the tube.
4 Bend the ends of the wire to secure the handle.
5 Glue the button in position as a base.
6 Bend the arm of the eye upwards and glue it to the front of the tube as another handle.

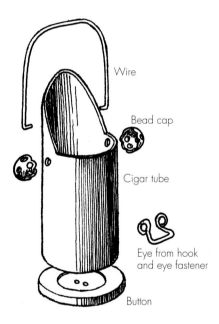

Wire

Bead cap

Cigar tube

Eye from hook and eye fastener

Button

Materials
Cigar tube or small cylinder
Brass wire
Small bead caps x 2
Flat button, just larger than diameter of cigar tube
Eye from hook and eye fastener

Cutting Tubes
Before cutting a tube, insert something into it to stop it from buckling. The easiest way to cut harder tubes, like cigar tubes, is to score them first with a modeller's saw, and then cut along the line with scissors.

Henryetta Lot

Henryetta Lot is a maid of all work. She is to be found in the alley, where she does the washing, the ironing, the gofering and, since the oven was moved into her realm, any cooking that is required and the washing up!

I varied my usual practice of doll making for Henryetta by first shaping the hands and arms in Fimo. I did this around a pipe cleaner so that I could attach them easily. I used a cotton ball for the head and filled it out with Polyfilla. For the bun I used nylon hair, and the doll itself I made with pipe cleaners.

Henryetta Lot's oven

In the early days of Nearly Court, the bar supplied all the refreshments and the staff seemed content with gin. This arrangement was fine until one of the guests asked for a hot snack! There was no room for a kitchen, so an oven was moved into the alleyway and food was provided from there.

Method

1 Remove the centre struts from both buckles, and file down any roughness.
2 Cut the zoo railing to fit under the large buckle, to make bars. Glue in place.
3 Mount two lengths of the triangular wood strip on the box so that they splay outwards.
4 Glue the zoo railing and its buckle frame onto wood strips.
5 Cut arches from the base of the box sides to give feet, and reinforce inside the box with balsa.
6 Use the small buckle as a door and glue in place.
7 File one side of the pot and lid flat, and stick it to the side of the oven, at the bottom.
8 Place the small chain link on the front panel.
9 Spray paint the oven and the scrabble tile black.
10 Glue a watch winder to the front of the scrabble tile, and set the tile under the stove top as a grill tray.
11 Use another watch winder for the oven door handle.
12 Attach a watch winder to a length of the brass wire and mount this on the chain link. Fix the link to the side of the oven.

13 Cut the curtain ring in half and glue one half from the link to the side of the oven, at the end opposite the watch winder.

14 Glue the other half of the ring horizontally, across the same side.

15 Cut the tiny round chain link in half, and support this with the blocked link to make a gauge.

16 Fix the last watch winder to the side of the oven, below the brass wire.

Materials
35mm film box
Large rectangular buckle
Small rectangular buckle
Toy zoo railings (commercial)
Triangular wood strip
Balsa
Little plastic pot and lid (commercial)
Scrabble tile
Watch winders or bead caps x 4
Brass wire
Chain link
Metal curtain ring
Tiny link (e.g. as found between necklace beads)
Solid chain link
Small fancy chain link

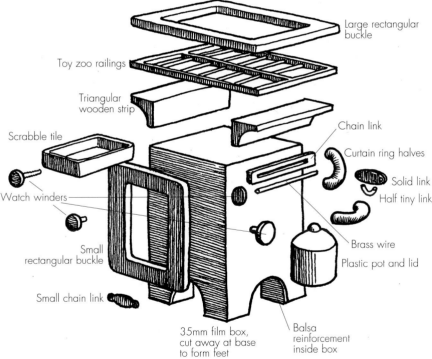

Large rectangular buckle

Toy zoo railings

Triangular wooden strip

Scrabble tile

Chain link

Curtain ring halves

Solid link

Half tiny link

Watch winders

Small rectangular buckle

Small chain link

Brass wire

Plastic pot and lid

35mm film box, cut away at base to form feet

Balsa reinforcement inside box

Easy Saucepans
Look in shops that sell plumber's supplies and you will find all sorts of treasures: copper cylinders which make lovely scale boilers and brass rings just asking to be made into saucepans! These rings are called olives. Top each olive with a brass button, shaft uppermost, and you've got a saucepan for pence! For the handle use a solid chain link, complete with jump ring. Just bend the end that doesn't have the ring and glue it to the side of the pan.

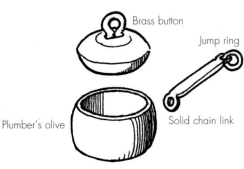

Brass button

Jump ring

Plumber's olive

Solid chain link

Iron and stand

There is practically no making in these. The real work lies in finding the wherewithall. What you need is a particular type of belt; the type that has a thin belt or belt end on top of a thicker one, and the ends finished with metal triangles.

Method

1 Insert pieces of card to fill up the openings of the metal triangles.
2 Cover the larger triangle with silver foil.
3 Cut two short pieces of card for the handle and paint them silver.
4 Glue these pieces of card to the top of the small triangle.
5 Cut a length of straw to fit between the card pieces and glue it in position.

Materials
Card
Large metal belt end
Small metal belt end
Silver foil
Drinking straw

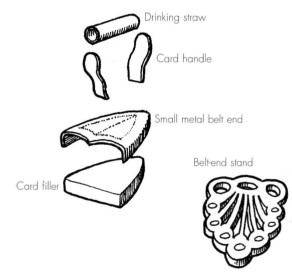

Drinking straw

Card handle

Small metal belt end

Belt-end stand

Card filler

Henryetta's toaster

This toaster's appearance may be fiddly, but its construction isn't. Simple cutting and gluing is all that is required here.

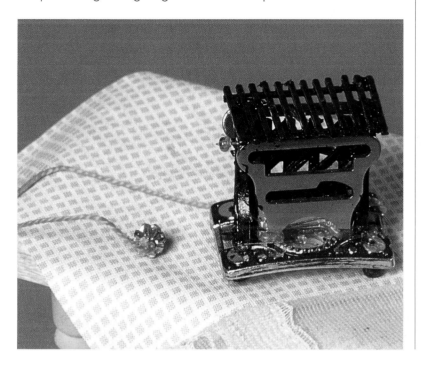

Method

1　Cut across the stocking suspender as shown.
2　Mount the square link on four tiny bead feet.
3　Cut the stirrers down as shown and fit a piece of fencing between them.
4　Glue the tea stirrers to the link.
5　Stick another piece of fencing across the top of this.
6　Use the cut stocking suspenders for doors.
7　Thread a bead onto each pin and glue one to the top of each door.
8　Attach a small bead cap to each end of a length of wire and glue one of the bead caps to the side of the toaster.

Easy Table
A table like this is so easy to make. All you need is a piece of balsa, cut to the size you require, and four bannister rods or turned wooden legs to support it.

Materials
Stocking suspenders x 2
　(metal part only)
Tiny black beads x 4
Square metal bracelet link
Plastic tea stirrers x 2
Fencing, gauge 00
　(commercial)
Tiny coloured beads x 2
Pins x 2
Twine
Small bead caps x 2

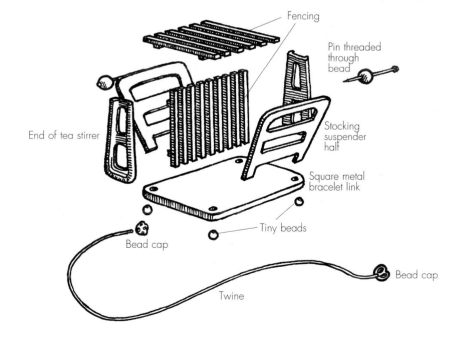

Fencing

Pin threaded through bead

End of tea stirrer

Stocking suspender half

Square metal bracelet link

Tiny beads

Bead cap

Bead cap

Twine

13 Sheila Blige's Bedroom

It was in character that Miss Blige choose a bold pattern for her wallpaper so the paper I used was a patterned giftwrap, bought from a stately home no less. For the carpet I was lucky enough to find one sample that fitted the whole room with no spaces left.

Four-poster bed

Isn't it about time you made your bed! If you can find a nurse's buckle or something similar, you can have fancy decorations, but basically this is an ordinary bed with a canopy added.

Method

1 Cut a base for the bed from card, and a second piece the same size to upholster as a mattress.

2 Make a footboard frame from card and attach half the buckle to this.

3 Use a taller piece of card for the headboard, place the other buckle half near its base, and draw around it.

4 Cut the buckle shape out a little smaller than the outline and glue the buckle over it.

5 Cut a hole from the card just above the buckle. Cover the card with pieces of cloth and thread them through the hole to give a ruched effect. Disguise the hole with the stud earring, and finish the canopy with curtains hanging from the sides.

6 Attach pillars, made from a home perm curler topped with a bead, at either side of both the head and footboards. Extend the headboard pillars with cocktail fork handles.

7 Assemble all three parts of the bed and stick them together.

8 Use a rectangle of card for the canopy and frame it with small pieces of balsa.

9 Glue a row of plastic tags to the balsa, and trim the corners with the 'M's from McDonalds' tea stirrers.

10 Spray paint the bed and canopy.

11 Run the notched strip around the canopy, and stick the jewellery piece to its front.

12 If you would like extra decoration, place beads in bead caps above the canopy corners.

13 Fix the upholstered mattress to the bed base.

14 Make up the bedding and bolster.

Materials

Card, firm
Nurse's belt buckle
Home perm curlers x 4
Beads x 4
Cocktail forks x 2
Balsa
Plastic tags that hold medicine capsules
McDonalds' plastic tea stirrers x 2
Small bead caps x 2
Small beads x 2
Notched wood strip
Small brooch
Card, light
Wadding
Cloth
Fancy stud earring
Lampshade gimp
Embroidery silk

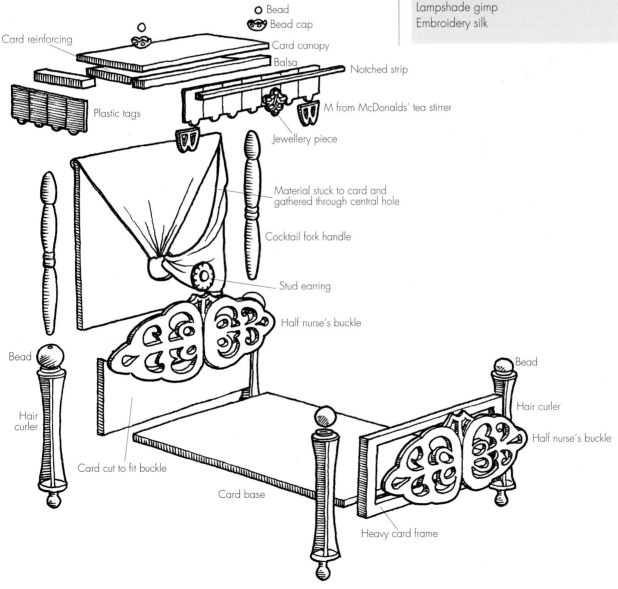

Bead
Bead cap
Card reinforcing
Card canopy
Balsa
Notched strip
Plastic tags
M from McDonalds' tea stirrer
Jewellery piece
Material stuck to card and gathered through central hole
Cocktail fork handle
Stud earring
Half nurse's buckle
Bead
Bead
Hair curler
Hair curler
Half nurse's buckle
Card cut to fit buckle
Card base
Heavy card frame

Chinese sideboard

A very ornate piece! Save beads, links, curlicues and clasps for this.

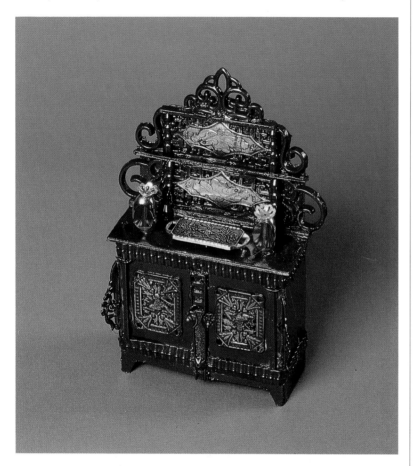

Method

1 Cut out the shape shown from the card.
2 Score as indicated by the dotted lines, and bend the card to form a box.
3 Reinforce the corners with more card.
4 Cut out and attach the back panel.
5 Glue the rectangular links to the front panel as doors, and the fancy links to the back panel for decoration.
6 Glue the longer shelf in place between the links on the back panel and the shorter shelf across the top of the back panel.
7 Cut a top from the card to overlap the cupboard at the front and sides.
8 Run lengths of beads, still on the string, along the sides of both buckles on the back panel.
9 Decorate the sides of each shelf on the back panel with curlicues.
10 Use the top half of the tea stirrer as a divider between the two cupboard doors.
11 Stick the pins through the beads and then through the cupboard front on either side of the curve at the base of the stirrer.

Materials
Card, firm
Rectangular metal bracelet or belt links x 2
Fancy metal bracelet links x 2
String of beads
Curlicues x 4 (e.g. from a plastic picture frame)
Plastic tea stirrer
Pins x 2
Small beads x 2
Corrugated metal strip (e.g. as used by flower arrangers)
Three-into-one necklace clasp
Jewellery pieces
Small bead cap

12 Run lengths of the corrugated metal
strip around the top and bottom of
the cupboard.
13 Top the whole sideboard with the
necklace clasp.
14 Decorate the sides of the cupboard
with the jewellery pieces.
15 Glue a bead cap to the cut end of
the plastic stirrer, in line with the
lower corrugated metal strip.
16 Cut a strip of card to fit across the
join of the back panel and cupboard
top, and glue it in place.

Necklace clasp

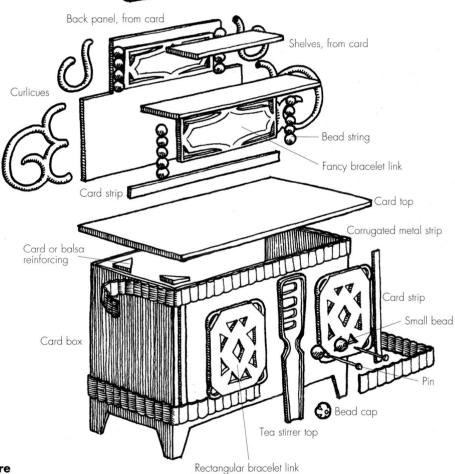

Back panel, from card

Shelves, from card

Curlicues

Bead string

Fancy bracelet link

Card strip

Card top

Corrugated metal strip

Card or balsa
reinforcing

Card strip

Small bead

Card box

Pin

Bead cap

Tea stirrer top

Rectangular bracelet link

Vases
**Vases are very easy to
make. For the vases here
I threaded pins through
bead caps and then glass
beads.**

Canterbury

It can be difficult to find matching items to make up a set, or to use in a piece of furniture. I solved that problem here by using the segments of a fan.

Method

1 Make up a small box from the card.
2 Cut two shelves from the card, slightly larger than the top of the box.
3 Glue one shelf to the top of the box.
4 Cut three segments of equal height from the fan and trim to the shape you want.
5 Place the three segments upright, one at either side and one in the centre of the box, and glue them in place.
6 Glue the second shelf across the top of the fan segments.
7 Run the square chain in three rows across the front of the shelves and the box.
8 Bend the filigree metal strip to go around the sides and back of the shelf top and trim to fit.
9 Insert the map pins at each corner of this metal strip.
10 Glue the beads under the box for feet.
11 Decorate the front of the box with the small link.
12 If you would like, add further decorations to the front and sides of the box with jewellery pieces and metal strip.
13 Spray paint.

Map pin

Filigree metal strip

Top shelf

Section cut from plastic fan

Overlapping top

Basic box

Square chain

Beads

Small bracelet link

Materials
Card, medium
Plastic filigree fan
Square chain
Filigree metal strip
Map pins
Beads x 4
Small bracelet link

Lacquered cabinet

The trick here is to use decorations cut from giftwrap. If you can't cut the pattern out easily, it is possible to paint out unwanted bits with black felt-tip pen.

Method

1 Make up the back and sides of the cabinet, and insert a card shelf halfway up the back.
2 Cut a card panel which goes two-thirds of the way to the top of the back panel.
3 Use the row of rounded railing arches as pigeon holes along the screen top.
4 Cut a central arch from the panel and use part of the circular earring to frame it.
5 Make drawer fronts with card pieces.
6 Fix the panel on the shelf.
7 Use card for the cabinet front, and make doors by cutting around three sides only. Score the hinge side of the doors and half open them. Do not stick the front on yet.

Materials

Card, firm
Circular drop earring
Plastic toy zoo fencing
Plastic tea stirrers x 2
Large bead cap
Oval bead
Plastic cocktail fork
Map pins x 12
Decorative giftwrap
Small bead caps x 2
Tiny rings x 4 (e.g. as found between beads of a necklace)

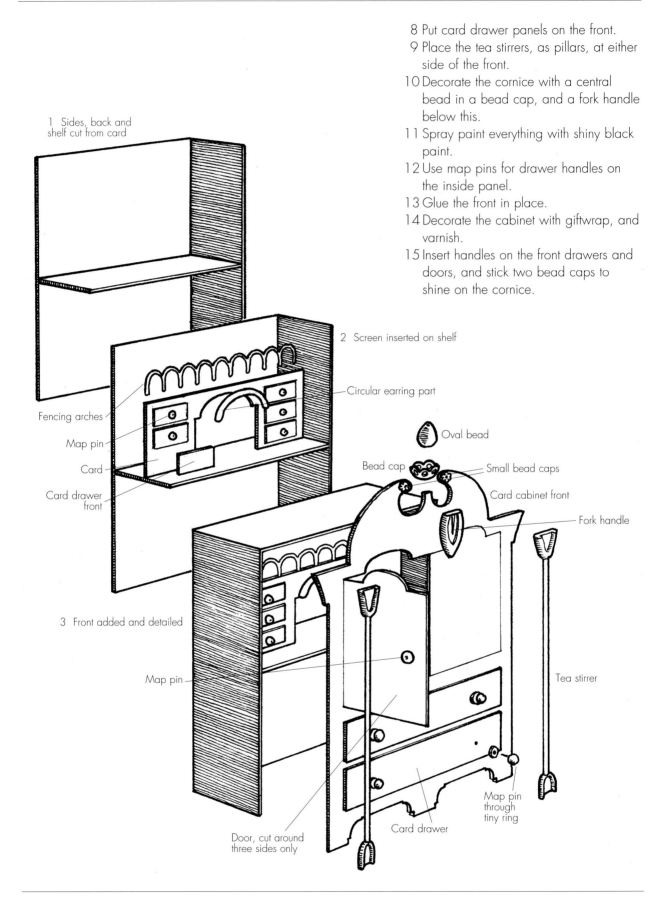

8 Put card drawer panels on the front.

9 Place the tea stirrers, as pillars, at either side of the front.

10 Decorate the cornice with a central bead in a bead cap, and a fork handle below this.

11 Spray paint everything with shiny black paint.

12 Use map pins for drawer handles on the inside panel.

13 Glue the front in place.

14 Decorate the cabinet with giftwrap, and varnish.

15 Insert handles on the front drawers and doors, and stick two bead caps to shine on the cornice.

1 Sides, back and shelf cut from card

2 Screen inserted on shelf

Fencing arches

Map pin

Card

Card drawer front

Circular earring part

Oval bead

Bead cap

Small bead caps

Card cabinet front

Fork handle

3 Front added and detailed

Map pin

Tea stirrer

Door, cut around three sides only

Card drawer

Map pin through tiny ring

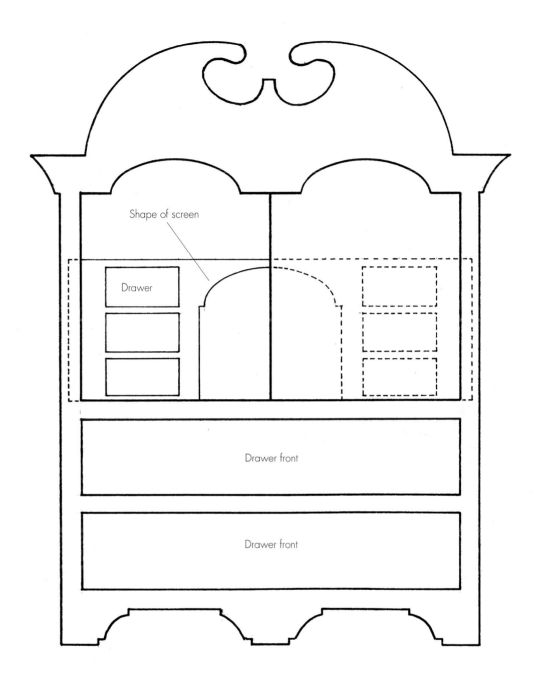

Shape of screen

Drawer

Drawer front

Drawer front

14 Maids' Common Room and Dormitory

There is never any shortage of giftwrap with William Morris designs, and they do make excellent wallpaper: one sheet is large enough to paper an entire room. For the carpet in the maids' room I used a face flannel which was cheap and had a nice pile to it. It even had fringed ends. For the mirror, I set a piece cut from a takeaway tin in a brooch frame.

Belt-buckle beds

Keep an eye out for interesting belt buckles! I was lucky enough to find a matching pair. Spoiled for choice, I wasn't sure whether to use one for a footboard and the other for a headboard, or whether to make a pair of matching beds. As I rather fancied making a dormitory for the girls, I opted for the latter. Beds are so easy to make I can't understand anyone buying them – when I overheard a woman buying an expensive kit at a dolls' house fair, I had to be physically restrained from shrieking advice at her! Well, it may be too late to tell her, but it's not too late to tell you.

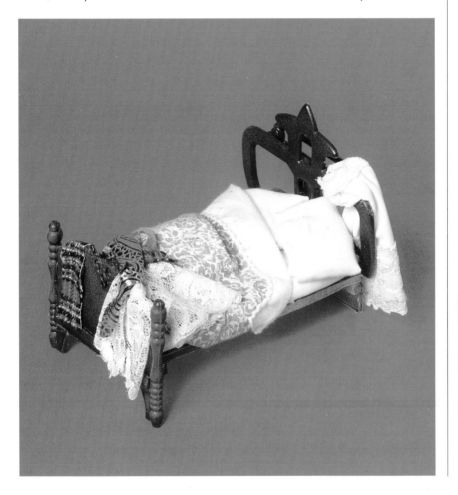

Method

1 Cut a strip of card to the width of the buckle and then cut this into four pieces, one each for the footboard, headboard, base and mattress. Cut an arch from the footboard and headboard to make legs.
2 Place the buckle on the headboard card and trace around its outline and details.
3 Cut out the panel details from the card.
4 Glue the buckle to the card backing.
5 Cut the prongs from the cocktail forks. The handles will be used as bedposts.
6 Cut a shape from the footboard card to take the necklace clasp and glue it in position.
7 Stick the footboard to the bedposts.

Materials

Belt buckle
Card, firm
Cocktail forks x 2
Three-into-one necklace clasp
Wadding
Cloth

8 Glue the headboard and footboard to
the base.

9 Spray paint brown.

10 Cut a piece of wadding to fit the
mattress card and a piece of cloth
slightly larger than this.

11 Place the wadding on the card and
cover it with the cloth.

12 Make small cuts along all sides of the
cloth, towards the card, and glue the
cloth to the reverse side of the card.

13 Place the mattress on the bed base.

14 Use scraps of fabric for the bedclothes,
and cover a piece of wadding to make
a pillow.

**Nightwear and Under
Garments
Use lace, fabric and
stocking trimmings to
make these. Drape them
over the beds to give
them a lived-in look.**

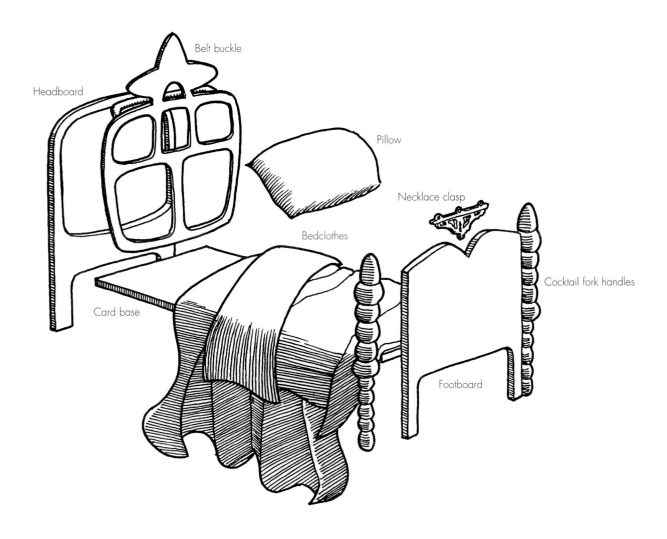

Belt buckle

Headboard

Pillow

Necklace clasp

Bedclothes

Cocktail fork handles

Card base

Footboard

Card table

The girls like to play cards in their spare time, so a card table has found its way into their dormitory. Unsure how to create cards of the right scale, I first set out the smallest cards I could find in a real game and photographed them, hoping the resulting print would reduce them to a ½ size. It didn't, so I resorted to mounting the original cards on paper and taking this to a photocopier where I had it reduced several times until the cards were scale size. When I got them home, I coloured them in and cut them out.

Materials
Card, firm
Balsa strip, 5mm (¼in)
Cocktail stirrers x 4
Woodgrain Contact or Fablon
Green baize or Fablon

Method
1. Cut a 90mm (3½in) table top from the card.
2. Reinforce the table top with the balsa strip, gluing it underneath.
3. Trim the cocktail stirrers to the height you want for the legs, and mount them under each corner.
4. Spray paint black.
5. Cover the table with the woodgrain Contact.
6. Cut a square of baize slightly smaller than the table top and glue it in place.
7. Arrange the cards and any other items you would like on the table.

Trays and Bottles
To make a tray, all you need is a solid belt link. Simply turn the ends of the link up and it's done! The bottles shown here are commercial ones and the glass is Biro casing cut down.

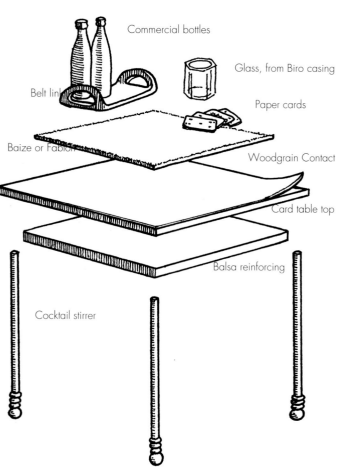

Commercial bottles

Glass, from Biro casing

Belt link

Paper cards

Baize or Fablon

Woodgrain Contact

Card table top

Balsa reinforcing

Cocktail stirrer

Gas fire

Find illustrations of tiles, in the size you require, to decorate this fireplace. Illustrations can always be reduced, but unless you have access to a colour photocopier, you will lose the colour scheme. Of course, colour can always be added later, with paint or felt-tip pins.

Method

1 Cut out the front of the Amplex box.
2 Spray paint black.
3 Trim the top curve of the opening with part of the earring.
4 Glue a small bead cap above the centre of the earring.
5 Place the stick-on furniture decorations across the bottom of the opening, flat.
6 Glue the bracelet link below the centre of the furniture decorations.
7 Trim the hairpiece or jewellery finding to fit inside the fireplace as a grate.
8 Stick a long link to either side of the opening, joining the earring and the furniture decorations.
9 Cut a piece of card to fit inside the doorframe, and cover it with tiles.
10 Cut a thin strip of card to fit the width of the doorframe.
11 Spray paint the doorframe and the thin strip of card.

Materials

Amplex box
Curved earring
Small bead cap
Stick-on furniture decorations x 2
Decorative bracelet link
Hairpiece or jewellery finding
Long, solid chain links x 2
Card, firm
Tile illustrations
Decorative picture frame

Attaching Maker's Nameplates
If you are using a plastic link for a maker's nameplate and the curve is wrong, put it in hot water for a few minutes. This will leave it malleable and you should be able to bend it to fit.

12 Fix the tiled card inside the frame.
13 Cut a card strip to sit across the top of the fireplace. Cover this with tiles.
14 Seat the gas fire in the doorframe assembly.
15 Cut the picture frame down to use as a hearth.
16 Cover a piece of card, cut to fit inside the hearth, with tiles.
17 Fix the card in place, and glue the hearth to the doorframe assembly.

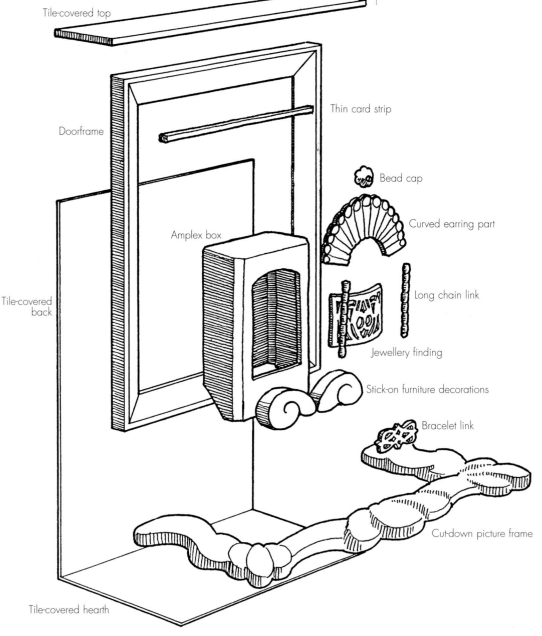

Tile-covered top

Doorframe

Thin card strip

Bead cap

Curved earring part

Amplex box

Long chain link

Tile-covered back

Jewellery finding

Stick-on furniture decorations

Bracelet link

Cut-down picture frame

Tile-covered hearth

15 Shower Room

T he shower room is long and deep so any detail at the back of the room is not clearly seen. In light of this, I decided just to give an impression and built a closed cupboard on the back wall, using chain links and eyes from hook and eye fasteners for handles. Above the cupboard I built shelves, the top ones holding the usual clutter of boxes, jars and books and the lower shelves stacked with linens and towels. At a charity shop I was lucky enough to find little lace-bound coasters. For linens I cut the coasters in half, glued each half around a piece of card and piled them, not too tidily, on the shelf. The towels I made by cutting short lengths off the arms and legs of babygrows. Real towel I found was too rough and frayed at the edges. For added detail I drew double lines at the end of each towel, with a felt-tip pen.

Shower unit

If you don't already use liquid detergent in your washing machine, have you thought of trying it? I do advocate it because it comes in a nice rectangular, opaque white container, and when you have made a dolls' house shower from the container, you may even find time to use the contents!

Materials

Bath
Rectangular plastic container
Drop earring
Stick-on furniture decorations
Card or plastic strip
Rectangular white plastic buckle

Shower Head
Brass wire
Fine plastic tube
Perforated disc (e.g. from beaded earring)
Galleried jewellery finding
Button
Bead cap
Bead, with hole big enough to take plastic tube
Stud earring bell

Pump
Large flat brass button
Small flat brass button
Lipstick case
Brass dress stud

Method

Bath
1 Cut across the container at the height you want the bath rim, bringing the back of the bath up to a suitable height.
2 Tailor the shape of the back to the earring you have chosen.
3 Top off the back of the bath with the drop earring.
4 Decorate the front and sides of the bath with the stick-on furniture decorations.
5 Run a strip of card or plastic behind the decorations as a bath rim.
6 Remove the centre strut from the buckle and cut the buckle in half.

Cutting Plastic Containers To cut a straight line around a plastic container, put an elastic band around it and draw a line where it lies, using a wax eyebrow pencil.

7 Glue the buckle halves under the bath as feet.

8 Spray paint silver.

Shower Head

1 Thread the wire through the plastic tube. This may require an element of force.

2 Cut the tube to the length you desire and bend it as shown.

3 The perforated disc is used for the shower head. With any luck, if you take a beaded earring apart you should find a perforated brass disc to which the beads were wired. This is perfect for the showerhead.

4 Mount the perforated disc in the galleried jewellery finding.

5 Glue the top of the button to the gallery.

6 Fix the bead cap to the centre of the button.

7 Place the bead on the bead cap, sideways on.

8 Top the whole unit with the earring bell.

9 Force the plastic tube through the earring bell and bead hole.

10 Attach the pipe to the earring drop on the back of the bath.

11 Spray paint silver.

Pump

1 Glue the small button to the large button.

2 Glue the lipstick case to the small button.

3 Top the pump with the dress stud.

4 Attach the pump to the side of the bath.

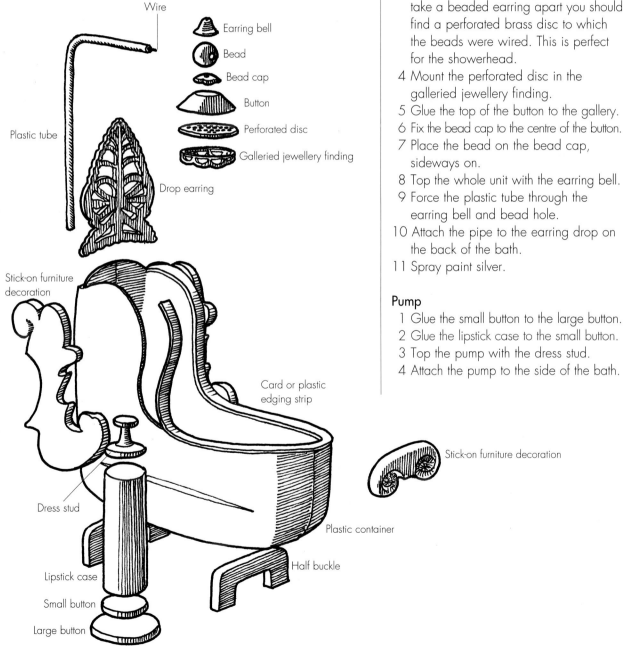

Wire

Earring bell

Bead

Bead cap

Button

Perforated disc

Galleried jewellery finding

Plastic tube

Drop earring

Stick-on furniture decoration

Card or plastic edging strip

Stick-on furniture decoration

Dress stud

Plastic container

Lipstick case

Small button

Large button

Half buckle

Jug stand

These are so easy to make. All you need is a fan and a button!

Method

1 Select the piece of fan you like and cut two matching lengths.
2 Stand the fan piece with the widest part at the base, tapering upwards.
3 Cut an arc at the bottom of each, keeping to the pattern.
4 Cut one piece in half, vertically.
5 Arrange the two cut halves either side of the whole piece, as shown, and glue them in place.
6 Top the stand with the button.
7 Spray paint white.

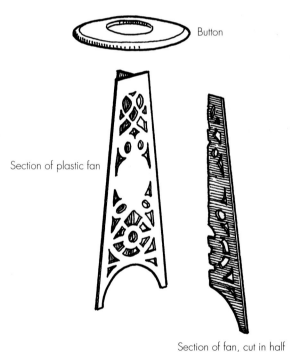

Button

Section of plastic fan

Section of fan, cut in half

Materials
Plastic filigree fan
Fancy button

16 Cupboard

This is more of a room than a cupboard really and still retains its own heating system, in the form of an appalling coal stove. However, since it was suggested that it would make a convenient storage room, it has become the dumping ground for all the pub's odds and ends. It now houses a vacuum cleaner, a carpet sweeper, a cot – all sorts of things.

Stove

Next time you go on an aeroplane, choose your airline according to the miniature drink bottles they provide. Their interesting shapes can be put to good use as stoves! However, if you are not going anywhere and have resorted to aspirin to mask your disappointment, you can use the bottle they come in instead.

Materials
Small box (optional)
Card, firm
Aspirin, miniature drink, or shampoo bottle
Small rectangular metal links x 2
Belt-hole eyelets x 2
Large rectangular metal link
Pins x 2
Embossed foil strip or metal necklace
Fancy necklace clasp
Felt-tip pen
Curtain ring
Christmas tree light holder
Washer (optional)

Method
1 Find a small box, or make one from card, to fit the front of your chosen bottle.
2 Cut a card top to overhang the box and glue it in place.
3 Glue a small metal link to the card top.
4 Mount the front of the box on the two belt-hole eyelets.
5 Glue the large metal link to the front of the box, and glue the remaining small metal link below it, to form doors.
6 Stick the back of the box to the front of the bottle.
7 Place the bottle and attached front on the card, trace around the bottle and extend the shape a little in front. Cut this shape out.
8 Fix the bottle and front to this card base.
9 Trim the raw edges of the base with the embossed foil or necklace.
10 Use the necklace clasp for a maker's nameplate.
11 Thread the pen through the curtain ring and Christmas tree light holder, and insert it into the bottle top. Use a washer to secure it if it doesn't fit.
12 If you would like some further decoration, trim the bottom edge of the light holder with embossed foil strip.
13 Spray paint black.

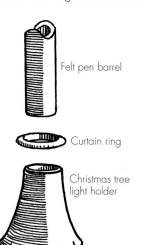

Felt pen barrel

Curtain ring

Christmas tree light holder

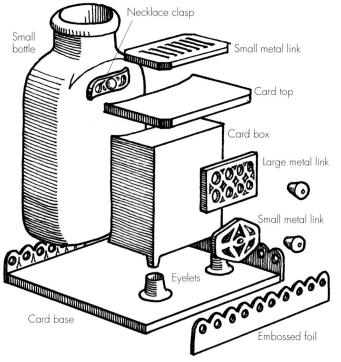

Small bottle

Necklace clasp

Small metal link

Card top

Card box

Large metal link

Small metal link

Eyelets

Card base

Embossed foil

Vacuum cleaner

If you have a metal tube, bend the nozzle around to fit into the bottle top.

Materials

Safety razor
Small metal locket
Brass washer (optional)
Press studs x 3
Stud earring bell
Metal bottle top
Small glue, paint or make-up tube
Three-into-one necklace clasp
Biro casing
Thin knitting needle
Jump rings x 2
Fine chain
Twine or fine cord
Small black bead
Bead cap

Method

1 Cut the head off the razor, at an angle.
2 Remove the hinge from the locket to separate the two halves.
3 Use the half with the chain link to back the razor head. I used a brass washer in between.
4 Use the second half of the locket for the trolley and add the press studs for wheels and the earring bell as a stand.
5 Glue the metal bottle top to the back of the front locket and mount this whole assembly onto the trolley, leaving room for the tube nozzle to fit behind it.
6 Cut the tube to fit, from the flat end rather than the nozzle end, and mount it on the trolley, behind the bottle-top assembly.
7 Glue the necklace clasp to the tube top.
8 Cut the knitting needle to the right length.
9 Attach the fine chain to the jump ring.
10 Thread the jump ring onto the knitting needle.
11 Cut a tiny length from the Biro casing and thread this onto the knitting needle, below the jump ring.
12 Glue the knitting needle in place in front of the tube.
13 Attach the loose end of the chain to the top of the front locket.
14 Decorate the razor front with the remaining press stud.
15 Thread a bead cap and the small button onto the twine or cord, secure one end with a knot, and glue the other end to the back of the tube.

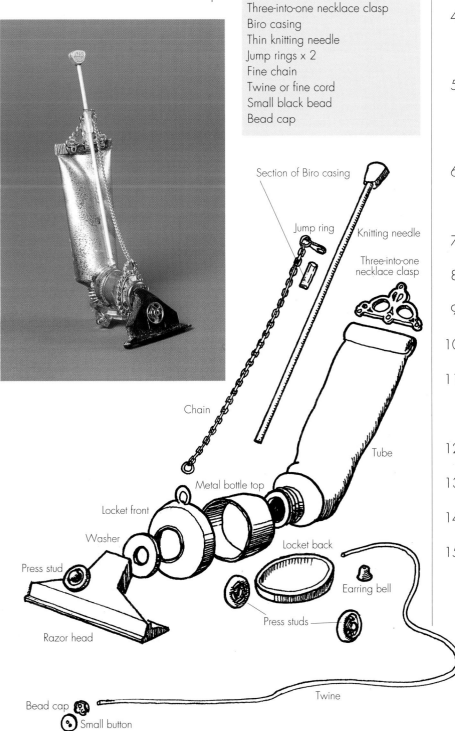

Section of Biro casing

Jump ring

Knitting needle

Three-into-one necklace clasp

Chain

Tube

Metal bottle top

Locket front

Washer

Locket back

Press stud

Earring bell

Razor head

Press studs

Bead cap

Small button

Twine

Carpet sweeper

Everyone had one of these, and although they redistributed dust rather than removing it, no-one threw them away – we've still got one!

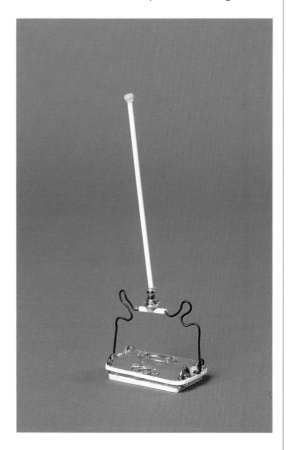

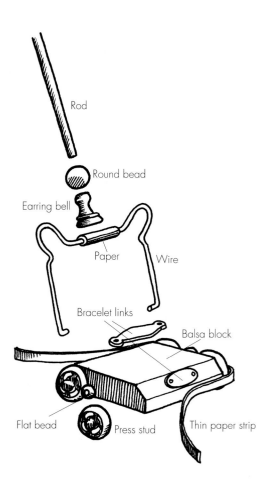

Materials
Balsa block 30 x 20 x 6mm
  (1³⁄₁₆ x ²⁵⁄₃₂ x ⁷⁄₃₂in)
Flat beads x 2
Press studs x 4
Small bracelet links x 2
Black Fablon or baize (optional)
Rod 2 x 90mm (¹⁄₁₆ x 3⁹⁄₁₆in)
Round bead
Stud earring bell
Bugle bead (optional)
Wire
Strip of paper 2mm (¹⁄₁₆in)
Small bead (optional)

Method
1 Turn the balsa block on its side and cut angles along both long sides.
2 Glue a flat bead to each side in the centre.
3 Bore a hole through each bead to take the handle wire.
4 Attach press studs as wheels either side of the flat beads.
5 Band around the block with the strip of paper.
6 Glue the tiny bracelet links in place, one on the centre front and the other on the block top, as a maker's nameplate.
7 Seat the rod in the round bead, add the bell, and glue in place.
8 Thread the bugle bead onto wire, or wind a small piece of paper around it.
9 Bend wire to look like Dennis the Menace's knees.
10 Glue the bell to the wire. Use a splodge of glue to make up the difference. This is easy if you use a glue gun, and it won't show – promise!
11 Insert the bent ends of the wire into the holes in the central beads.
12 Top the rod with a small bead or leave it plain.

Baby's cot

I would say it is doubtful whether plastic fans are all that good for moving air around, but they do have wonderful tracery, which is a boon to modellers. You will find it cuts quite well with scissors if you cut one twirl at a time.

Materials

Filigree plastic fan
Small plastic dish or box (airline food dishes are perfect)
Plastic rings x 2
Miniature ladder (commercial)

Method

1 Peruse your fan and choose which pieces you would like as cot sides. Cut two.
2 Glue the fan pieces either side of the box so that they sit a little above its rim.
3 Cut a section from each plastic ring to top each fan piece, and glue in place.
4 Cut the ladder to fit between the legs and glue it in place to form a shelf.
5 Spray paint.

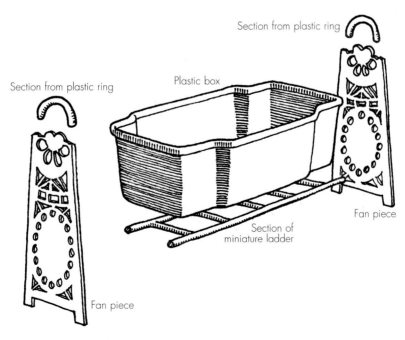

Section from plastic ring

Section from plastic ring

Plastic box

Fan piece

Section of miniature ladder

Fan piece

17 Accounts Room

Ben Tizzy is a long-term resident of the boarding house. He gives his services as an accountant in lieu of rent. He has actually moved into the accounts room where he has his bed, a safe, roll-top desk, and a flat desk complete with typewriter!

Ben's hot-water bottle

Just the thing for Tizzy's tootsies!

Method

1 Place the balsa in the top third of a biggish piece of the plastic material.
2 Glue generously all over the balsa.
3 Draw up the lower portion of the plastic so that it covers the balsa, and press down all the edges so that they are glued and flat.
4 Draw the outline of a hot-water bottle around the edges of the balsa and another larger outline around this. It is the larger outline that you will cut around.
5 Before you cut it out, punch holes at the top and bottom of the bottle and at the side to form a handle. A leather punch is ideal for this.
6 Cut out the bottle, being generous at the top end where the plug will go, and cutting a higher piece at the back to take in the hole.
7 Force open the top of the water bottle and reinforce the opening with a tiny circle of card.
8 Force part of the chain link through the card and into the bottle to form a stopper.
9 Cut a piece of plastic to go around the neck of the bottle, and cut another sliver of plastic and glue this to the neck of the bottle for the maker's nameplate.

Materials

Balsa, small square
Plastic (e.g. from an old handbag or bean bag)
Card
Long chain link

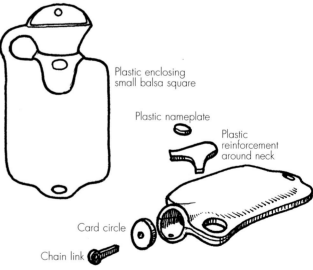

Plastic enclosing small balsa square

Plastic nameplate

Plastic reinforcement around neck

Card circle

Chain link

Ben Tizzy's bed

In other projects I have used belt buckles and bracelet links to give matching foot and headboards – for this bed I used haircombs.

Materials
Balsa
Card, medium
Haircombs x 2
Home perm curlers x 4
Beads x 4
Large beads x 4 (optional)
White handkerchief
Wadding
Material

Method
1 Cut a rectangle of balsa to make a bed base.
2 Cut a piece of card the same size to top it.
3 Trim the ends of the balsa and the card to fit the curve of the combs.
4 Glue the combs to either end of the balsa base.
5 Glue home perm curlers to the sides of the combs as bedposts.
6 Top each curler with a bead.
7 If the bed is too low, glue a bead under each foot.
8 Glue a strip of card across the teeth at the base of each comb.
9 Spray paint brown.
10 Cut the hanky in half.
11 Cut a piece of wadding to fit the card.
12 Place the wadding on the card and one half of the hanky over this.
13 Make little cuts towards the card, around all sides of the hanky, and glue the hanky segments to the reverse side of the card.
14 Make a pillow with wadding and part of the other half hanky.
15 Use the remaining piece of hanky for a sheet.
16 Cut a piece of thicker, coloured material for a blanket.

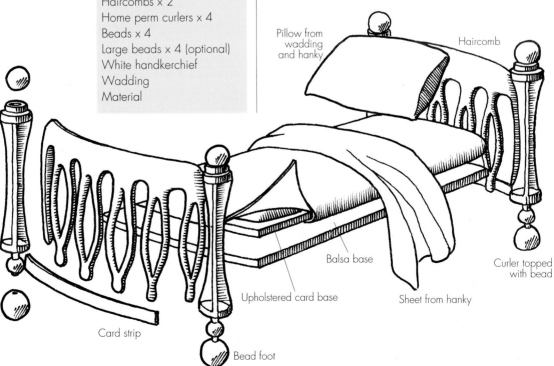

Pillow from wadding and hanky

Haircomb

Balsa base

Curler topped with bead

Upholstered card base

Sheet from hanky

Card strip

Bead foot

Ben's typewriter

I cut rows of teeth from an old comb for my typewriter keys.

Materials
Card, thin
Card, firm
Woodgrain paper
Balsa
Dark paper
Small black comb
Ruler
Biro refill
Watch winders x 2
Drop earring mounts x 2
Gold wire
Small jewellery piece
Tiny gold rings (e.g. as found
  between necklace beads)
Small chain link

Method
1 Cut a base for the typewriter from the thin card.
2 Cut a piece from the firm card, slightly larger than the base.
3 Cover both pieces of card with the woodgrain paper.
4 Mount the thin card on the firm card.
5 Cut a step for the back of the typewriter from the balsa. You may like to cover it with dark paper.
6 Glue a strip of card along the teeth of the comb, about one-quarter of the way down.
7 Cut the teeth off along the base of this card.
8 Cut three small lengths from this for your three rows of keys.
9 Glue the balsa block to the back of the base.
10 Stand the three rows of keys in front of the block, stepping up each row with strips of card to form three tiers.
11 Cut a tiny sliver of ruler, with marked divisions on it, to the length of your rows of teeth.
12 Place the ruler piece behind the back row of teeth.
13 Cut two equal lengths of Biro refill and cover them with dark paper.
14 Glue one piece of refill on top of the other.
15 Stick a watch winder into each end of the top refill.
16 Make tabs for the bottom refill from the earring mounts.
17 Cut a length of the gold wire between the rollers.
18 Attach the jewellery piece to the centre of this wire.
19 Stick the roller assembly to the balsa block.
20 Glue another length of gold wire to the base of the front row of teeth.
21 Add the two tiny rings either side of the gold wire at the front.
22 Glue the chain link across the front of the base for a maker's nameplate.

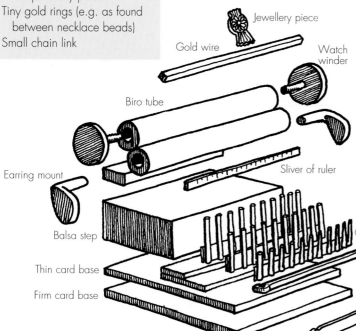

Jewellery piece

Gold wire

Watch winder

Biro tube

Sliver of ruler

Earring mount

Balsa step

Comb teeth with card strip backing

Gold wire

Thin card base

Firm card base

Small chain link

Safe

I am quite excited! In making this safe I have found a new modelling material. When you buy a packet of foil tins for freezing food, you get lids made of foil- covered card. These lids are the perfect material to make welded strips with rivets. Turn the lid so that the card side is uppermost and make indentations in the card with a needle. Use a ruler for guidance. You can make lots of strips up in advance, in single or double rows. If you want to make up a box or some other shape, score from the foil side and bend.

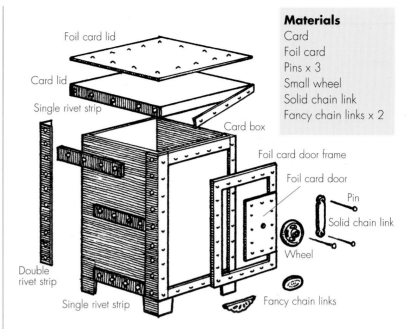

Foil card lid
Card lid
Single rivet strip
Card box
Foil card door frame
Foil card door
Pin
Solid chain link
Wheel
Double rivet strip
Single rivet strip
Fancy chain links

Materials
Card
Foil card
Pins x 3
Small wheel
Solid chain link
Fancy chain links x 2

Method

1. Make a box out of card as shown, scoring where indicated.
2. Cut a lid from heavy card that juts out all around, and glue in place.
3. Top this with a second lid made from foil card, with rivets punched all around the edges.
4. Make a door from foil card, and punch rivets around it.
5. Make a frame to fit around the door panel, and decorate it with rivets.
6. Bind each edge of the box with a double rivet strip.
7. Use single rivet strips to trim around the top and bottom of the safe. Trim around the face of the lid and across the centre of each side as well.
8. Make a hole in the centre of the door, then insert a pin through the wheel and into this hole.
9. Insert two pins into the solid chain link, and drill two more holes to take them.
10. Glue the fancy link in place, for the maker's nameplate.
11. Add the other link as detail, between the legs.
12. Spray paint silver or grey.

Box plan

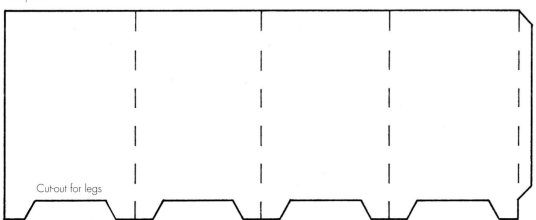

Cut-out for legs

Ben Tizzy's ink stand

This is so easy to make! Whittling the pencils takes the longest time.

Ledgers
Ledgers are all too easy to make. Simply use the back ends of cheque stubs! For a bill spike, secure a pin in a fancy button or bead cap. I cut tiny pieces of paper to spear onto it.

Letter Rack
To make a letter rack, simply bend a large metal drop earring to form two sides and a base. All you need do then, is cut tiny squares of paper to place in it.

Method

1 Whittle one end of the bamboo slivers to a pencil point and cut them to size.
2 Paint or colour the pencils.
3 Cut a sliver from the numbered part of the ruler, in proportion to your pencils.
4 Arrange the pencils and ruler in the cartridge case or sheath.
5 Glue the cartridge to the centre of the bracelet link.
6 Top each bead with a watch winder or bead cap.
7 Glue the beads either side of the pencil holder.
8 Cut a tiny piece from the eraser.
9 Place an extra pencil and the piece of eraser on the tray.

Materials
Bamboo slivers (e.g. from bamboo placemat)
Old ruler
Metal sheath from eyebrow pencil or small cartridge case
Bracelet link
Cut glass crystal beads x 2
Watch winders or bead caps x 2
Eraser

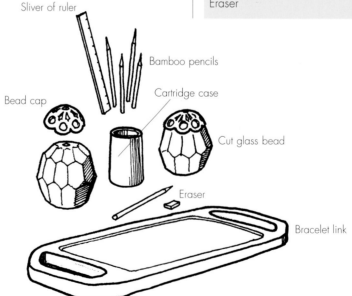

Sliver of ruler

Bead cap

Bamboo pencils

Cartridge case

Cut glass bead

Eraser

Bracelet link

Ben Tizzy's desk

A toy ladder topped with map pins gave this desk the impressive look I wanted. Simple fencing would do just as well.

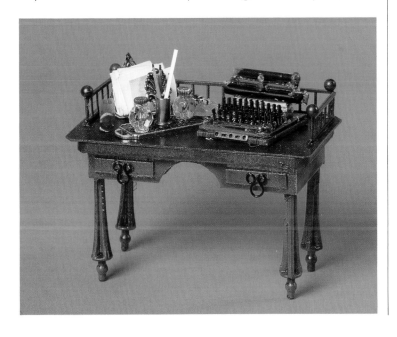

Method

1 Cut a desk top from the firm card.
2 Cut a piece, slightly larger, from the shiny card and cut the front corners square.
3 Reinforce the underside of the table with two strips of balsa.
4 Hide the wood by cutting strips of light card to fit the sides, back and front and gluing them in place.
5 Cut an arch from the front strip for leg room.
6 Cut the curlers to the height you want, and insert them into the balsa strips at each corner of the desk. Glue them in place.
7 Trim the ladder to fit the back and sides of the desk top.
8 Reinforce the ends and corners of the ladder with the map pins.
9 Cut two drawer panels from the light card, for the front of the desk, and glue them in place.
10 Spray paint.
11 Glue the eyes from the hook and eye fasteners to the drawer fronts, for handles.

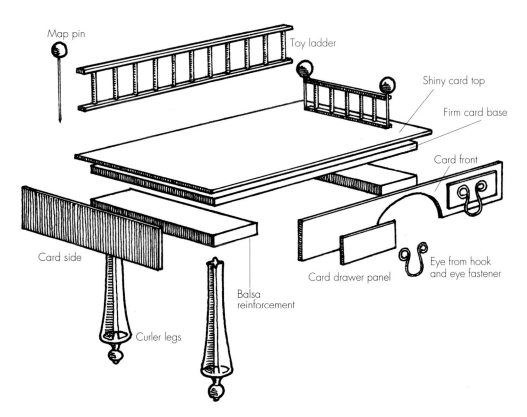

Materials
Card, firm
Card, shiny
Balsa
Card, light
Home perm curlers x 4
Toy ladder (e.g. as for model railways)
Map pins x 4
Eyes from hook and eye fasteners x 2

Wastepaper Basket
For a wastepaper basket, upend a thimble and fill it with torn and rumpled pieces of paper.

Roll-top desk

The curve of the roll top for this desk is supported by a toilet roll cylinder. The roll top itself is a bamboo placemat.

Method

1 Back the bamboo mat with paper to keep it together when you cut it.
2 Cut the toilet roll tube in half, downwards.
3 Cut the sides, base and back for the desk from heavy card, and assemble them.
4 Use balsa to make a top panel, and cover this with another panel of card.
5 Fit the toilet roll tube over the curved sides.
6 Cut the bamboo mat to fit over the tube, and glue in place.
7 Fit a card front above the roll top, and add drawers.
8 Add an apron below the roll top, complete with central arch and drawer fronts.
9 Make aprons for the sides, and a top for the desk.

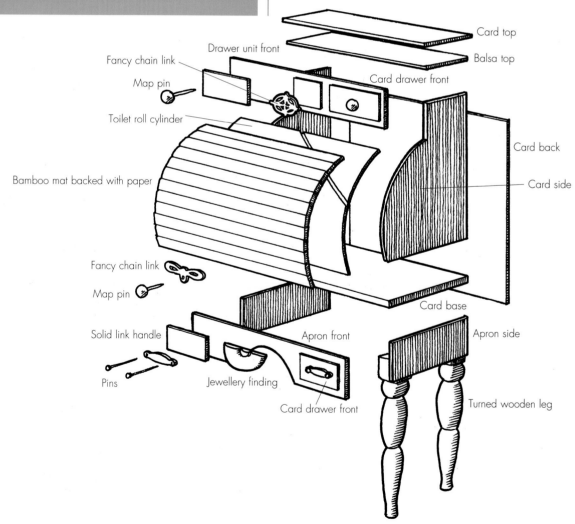

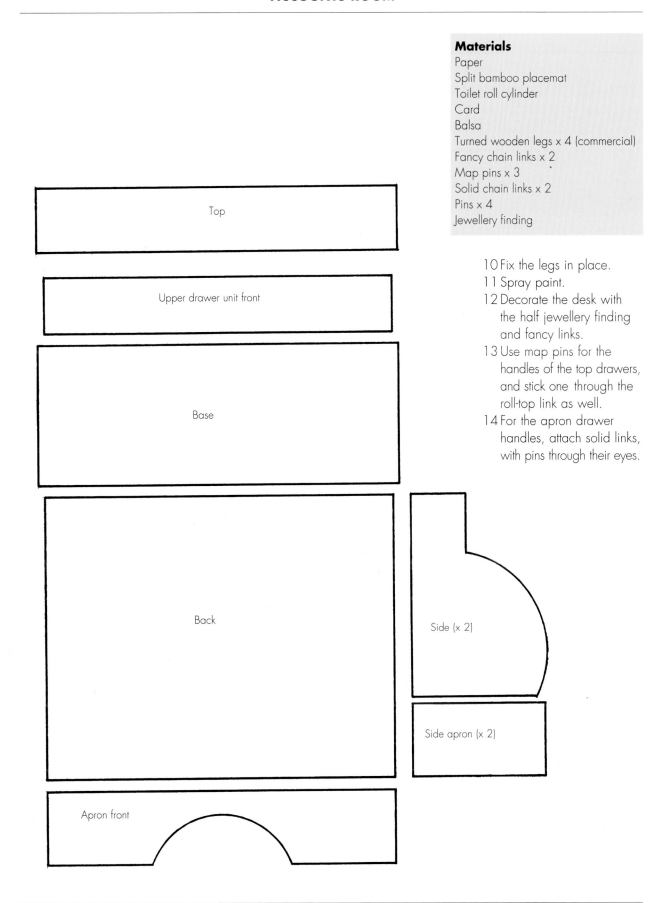

Materials
Paper
Split bamboo placemat
Toilet roll cylinder
Card
Balsa
Turned wooden legs x 4 (commercial)
Fancy chain links x 2
Map pins x 3
Solid chain links x 2
Pins x 4
Jewellery finding

10 Fix the legs in place.
11 Spray paint.
12 Decorate the desk with the half jewellery finding and fancy links.
13 Use map pins for the handles of the top drawers, and stick one through the roll-top link as well.
14 For the apron drawer handles, attach solid links, with pins through their eyes.

Top

Upper drawer unit front

Base

Back

Side (x 2)

Side apron (x 2)

Apron front

18 Conservatory

The conservatory is an extravaganza which really has more to do with stage design than with dolls' house making, but I love the Kew Gardens type of conservatory and have always wanted to make an ornate one in miniature. I realized early on in the enterprise that making it in ½ scale would mean moving to a larger house in order to fit it in, so I settled for ¼ scale.

My original idea was to use clear plastic bottles as domes, and it was while I was trying (unsuccessfully) to weld them together that fate sent me a parrot cage. I warded off all offers of parrots and budgies with commendable dignity and abandoned the bottles: my parrot cage would be transformed!

Half the fun of my idea of a conservatory was to make a plastic fan I had acquired into a spiral staircase, so I had to have a gallery and that, in turn, needed a circular railing.

My search for miniature dried plants led me to a garden centre and there I spied an underwater filter pump. Upon enquiry, I was assured that it would throw water in a scale-size fountain jet. It does!

The point about modelling something like this is that, providing you make your own figures to people the scene, scale doesn't really matter. When it came to making my people, I decided to make them one-dimensional and showy.

Conservatory structure

The whole concept for this conservatory revolved around a nice birdcage, but lots of other makings would have done as well. Having acquired the cage I used what came to hand: a lampshade frame, miniature plastic fencing, and bulb bowls with cutaway patterns around the tops. I'm confident you could change all these basic materials and still get a good effect.

Method

1 Remove the floor from the birdcage.
2 Cut the lampshade frame in half.
3 Arrange the lampshade halves either side of the birdcage but do not fix them in place yet.
4 Trace around the whole unit to find the size baseboard you will need, and cut a piece of plywood to fit.
5 Cut the lower front out of the birdcage.
6 Glue a strip of card around the bottom of both sides of the lampshade halves, to form walls.
7 Cover these walls with brick paper.
8 Cover the baseboard with Fablon.
9 Glue the fountain unit (*see* page 135) to the centre of the baseboard.
10 Wire the birdcage to the baseboard and to the steps of the fountain unit.
11 Cut the plant hanger so that it will go around the fountain and provide pillars to support the gallery.

Materials

Birdcage
Lampshade frame
Plywood
Card, thin
Brick paper
Fablon
Fountain unit (*see* page 135)
Small wire plant hanger
Electroplated nickel silver entree dish (with glass insert)
Card, firm
Home perm curlers x 2
Dolls' house fencing
Spiral staircase (*see* page 137)
Miniature garden fencing (commercial)
Plastic bulb bowls with fancy rims x 2
Plastic toy zoo fencing
Conservatory plants

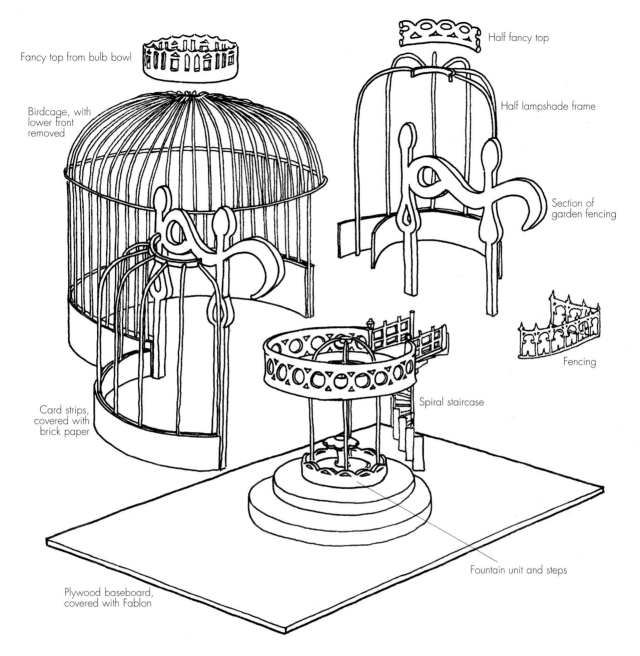

Fancy top from bulb bowl

Half fancy top

Birdcage, with
lower front
removed

Half lampshade frame

Section of
garden fencing

Fencing

Card strips,
covered with
brick paper

Spiral staircase

Fountain unit and steps

Plywood baseboard,
covered with Fablon

12 Turn the hanger upside down so
that the open part fits over the
fountain and the mesh base makes
a see-through centre for the gallery.

13 Place the entree dish on the firm
card and trace around it.

14 Form a base from card to replace
the glass plate of the entree dish.
This will form the gallery floor.

15 Cut a circle from the centre of the
card to allow a view of the fountain
below. Fix it in place.

16 Remove a section of the side from
the entree dish to allow for a
walkway to the stairs.

17 Trim the curlers and fix one either side
of the gap in the gallery.

18 Spray paint the gallery white.

19 Glue the gallery in place, resting
on the plant hanger.

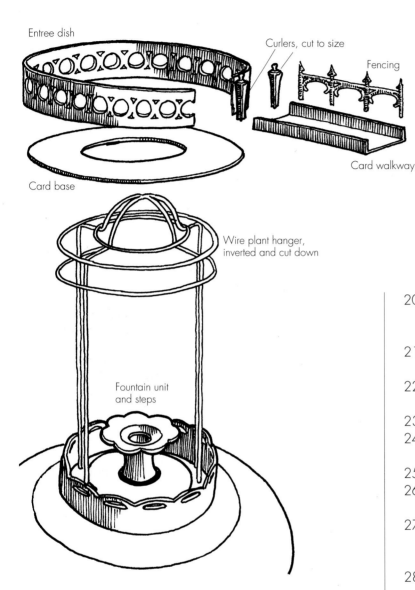

Entree dish

Curlers, cut to size

Fencing

Card walkway

Card base

Wire plant hanger,
inverted and cut down

Fountain unit
and steps

20 Make a spiral staircase (*see* page 137)
   to the height of the gallery floor. Put it in
   place but do not fix it yet.
21 Cut a card walkway to reach from the
   gallery to the staircase.
22 Score and bend up the sides of the
   walkway to fit the top step of the staircase.
23 Reinforce the walkway if necessary.
24 Cut lengths of fencing to fit along the
   sides of the walkway.
25 Glue the spiral staircase in place.
26 Now attach the lampshade halves to the
   birdcage with glue and wire.
27 Cut pillars from the miniature garden
   fencing and disguise the raw edges of
   the cage with them.
28 Remove the fancy tops from the small
   bulb bowls. Use one as a crown for the
   top of the birdcage. Cut the other in
   half, and use these halves as crowns for
   the tops of the lampshade halves.
29 Fence around the top step and the front
   of the conservatory with plastic toy fencing.
30 Decorate the conservatory with plants
   (*see* page 148).

Working model fountain

Using a water aerator is all very well, but it does have to be sunk in a bowl of water. The first thing to do here then, is to find a bowl to fit it. A plastic one is preferable because it is light and because it is easy to cut a hole in it to thread the lead through. It is always best to test the filter in water before you fix it in.

Materials

Hollow cake columns of
  two sizes
Underwater filter
Plastic bowl
Small picnic plate
  (to fit bowl)
Card
Balsa strips
Fablon
Plastic bulb bowl with
  fancy rim

Method

1 Cut the bottom off the smaller cake column and glue it in position, making sure that its hollow tube is directly over the water outlet in the filter.
2 Seal all leaks!
3 Remove the flared top from the larger column, and top the smaller column with this.
4 Cut a nick for the lead at the top of the bowl.
5 Fix the filter to the bottom of the bowl and bring the lead through the nick at the top.
6 Cut a large hole in the centre of the plate.
7 Glue the plate over the bowl (you may need to trim it to fit) to deflect any stray water back in.

8 Make steps to disguise the filter's workings. To seat the fountain in the centre of the conservatory floor (*see* page 132), trace around the birdcage and cut a circular step to fit inside it.

9 Cut a hole from the centre of the step to take the fountain.

10 Raise the step by resting it on blocks of balsa.

11 Run a thin strip of card around the front of the step to hide the balsa.

12 Make several graduated steps this way until you reach the height you want.

13 Cover the steps with Fablon.

14 Cut the fancy rim off the bulb bowl and use this to make a circular fence around the fountain.

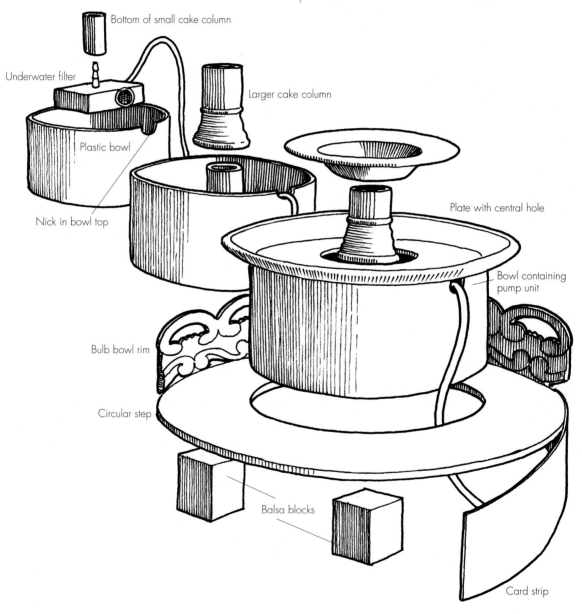

Bottom of small cake column

Underwater filter

Larger cake column

Plastic bowl

Nick in bowl top

Plate with central hole

Bowl containing pump unit

Bulb bowl rim

Circular step

Balsa blocks

Card strip

Spiral staircase

If you really fancy a spiral staircase, look for fans in jumble sales. They look just like wrought iron in miniature, and the segments even have the right shape for steps and banisters. One fan is plenty for a short staircase, but the one I made has 14 steps and required two. Now comes the hardest part for me: describing a spiral staircase without using my hands!

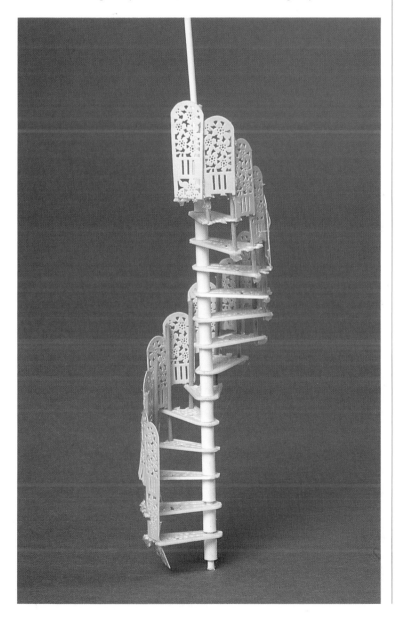

Method

1 Check that the rod fits snugly into your tubing.
2 Remove the rod and cut the tubing into 14, 10mm (⅜in) lengths (one for each tread).
3 Clamp the fan, still intact, with its segments one on top of the other, and cut them all together as shown.
4 Keeping them clamped, drill a hole through them all to take the rod. This needs to be a snug fit.
5 Drill a small hole in the far end of each segment to take the cocktail sticks. Again, this needs to be a snug fit.
6 Unclamp the fan segments and thread onto the rod one 'riser' (piece of tube) followed by one fan segment, in turn, until you reach the height you want for the staircase. End the staircase with a long length of tube to reach the full height.
7 To fix the staircase in the conservatory (*see* page 134), leave a small piece of rod jutting down at the bottom, to insert into a hole in the baseboard.
8 Turn the fan segments around the shaft to form a spiral.
9 Glue a cocktail stick into place on each segment to support the banisters.
10 Using the third fan, fit an upright segment to each stick.
11 Glue the segments in place and trim the sticks to fit.
12 Position the staircase in the conservatory and mark the point on the baseboard that will take the rod at its base.

Materials
Plastic rod
Plastic tubing
Plastic filigree fans x 3 (2 identical)
Cocktail sticks

13 Remove the staircase, drill a hole at the point marked and replace the staircase, inserting the rod into the hole.

14 Arrange any greenery you would like around the staircase before you glue it in place. (*See* page 148.)

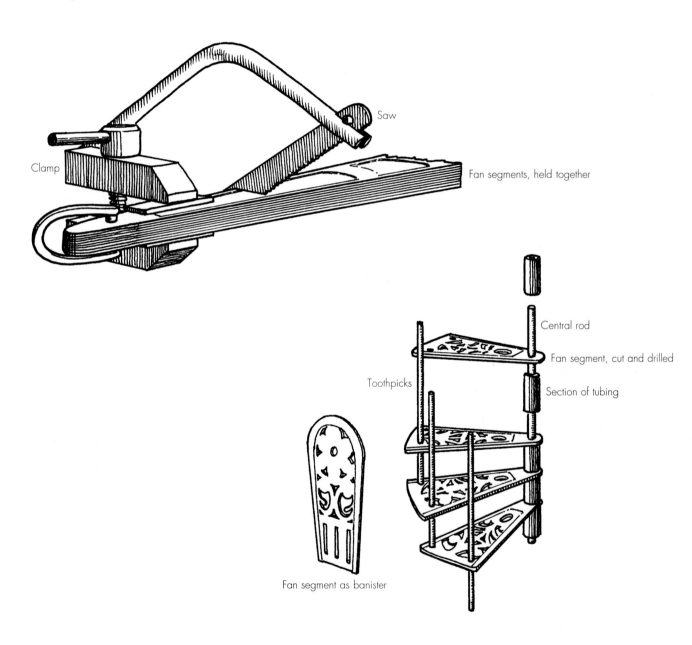

Saw

Clamp

Fan segments, held together

Central rod

Fan segment, cut and drilled

Toothpicks

Section of tubing

Fan segment as banister

Garden tables

If you are a pizza lover, choose your supplier with care and make sure you hit the right hut! The ones you want are those that use a three-pronged disc to hold the box lid off your pizza. The pizza is unimportant here, the pronged disc is almost a miniature table in itself!

Once you have collected a few of these pronged things, have a look in your collection for filigree brooches, buttons and bangles and you should be all set to create!

Method

Three-Legged Table

1 Use the disc for legs. Glue a bead to each prong for extra height if you wish.
2 Top the disc with a filigree brooch, removing any stones first.
3 If you want a shelf, insert the smaller brooch halfway up the legs, again removing any stones first.
4 Spray paint white.

Pedestal Table

1 If you are using a chesspiece, remove its head.
2 Glue the chesspiece or lipstick tube to the button or brooch.
3 Glue the brooch or buckle to the top of the chesspiece or lipstick tube.
4 If the brooch is too small, enclose it in a bangle.
5 If you use a buckle, fill in the centre with card.
6 Spray paint white.

Materials

Three-Legged Table
Three-pronged disc
   from takeaway pizza
Beads x 3 (optional)
Filigree brooch
Small filigree brooch (optional)

Pedestal Table
Chesspiece or lipstick tube
Button or brooch
Brooch or fancy buckle
Bangle (optional)
Card (optional)

Three-legged table

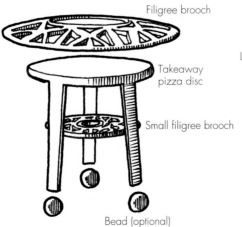

Filigree brooch

Takeaway
pizza disc

Small filigree brooch

Bead (optional)

Pedestal table

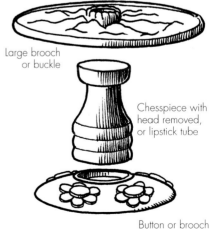

Large brooch
or buckle

Chesspiece with
head removed,
or lipstick tube

Button or brooch

Garden chairs

Here's where you fish out your dangle earrings. The best ones have a metal disc and then the dangle. You can use the disc as the chair 'cushion' and the dangle as the chair back.

You will also need some frogs. Not live ones! These plastic ones are used by flower arrangers to hold oasis in place. They have four legs and are perfect for stools. Both frogs and drawer handles can be bought in sets to make matching chairs. If you can't find matching pairs of earrings, links from a chain belt or bracelet, or fan segments, will give you a complete set.

Method

Four-Legged Chair

1 Use the frog for the chair base and top it with a button to neaten up the seat.
2 Bend the drop earring around a little to fit the curve of the seat and glue it in place as the chair back.
3 Now the chair looks nice, but is a little top-heavy. To avoid it toppling backwards, counterweight it by gluing something heavy under the front of the seat. I used little pieces of solder.
4 Spray paint white.

Pedestal Chair

1 Bend your chosen backpiece around a little to fit the curve of the drawer handle.
2 Glue the back to the drawer handle.
3 Spray paint white. You may need more than one coat.

Materials

Four-Legged Chair
Florist's frog
Button
Drop earring
Small scraps (for ballast)

Pedestal Chair
Earring, belt link or fan segment
Drawer handle

Pedestal chair

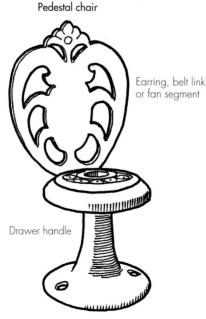

Earring, belt link or fan segment

Drawer handle

Four-legged chair

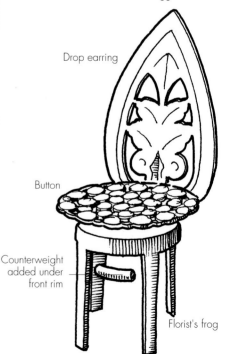

Drop earring

Button

Counterweight added under front rim

Florist's frog

19 Making Dolls

How you wish to use your dolls will influence the way you go about making them. I like to pose my dolls and have them grasp things in their hands, and I have evolved my own way of making them so that I can do this. For the little people in the conservatory, however, I didn't need this mobility, but I did want them to be bright and showy. Also, because of the set-up of the conservatory, I knew they would only be seen from one side, so when it came to making these dolls, I altered my usual methods.

Movable dolls

This is only one way of making dolls. Don't limit yourself with the materials you use. A head need not be a bead – it could be made from a cotton ball, filled out and given shape with Polyfilla.

Materials
Pipe cleaners
Beads or cotton balls
Cotton wool, embroidery
    cotton or nylon hair
Paint
Polyfilla

Male
Felt
Card
Fine fabric
White paper
Black paper

Female
Stiff paper
Fine fabric
Lace, narrow ribbon,
    tiny buttons etc.

Modelling with Fimo
I sometimes vary this practice of doll making by first shaping the hands and arms in Fimo. I always shape them around a pipe cleaner so that they are easy to attach.

Method
1 Make the basic body from pipe cleaners, wrapping them around each other to build up a solid form. Leave the arms long enough to bend the end of the pipe cleaner around. This gives the dolls hands that can grasp.
2 Use a bead for the head, building up a face with Polyfilla.
3 Paint or draw the facial features on.
4 Cotton wool, cotton or nylon hair are used for hair and whiskers.
5 Attach the head to the body after it has been dressed.

Bead head with cotton wool hair

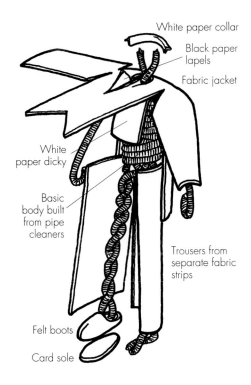

White paper collar

Black paper lapels

Fabric jacket

White paper dicky

Basic body built from pipe cleaners

Trousers from separate fabric strips

Felt boots

Card sole

Female

1 Place plenty of glue on the bead head and pile the cotton wool (or alternative) onto the glue while it is still wet.
2 Tease the cotton wool out into a long strand and twist the strand into a hair style.
3 Cut out the underskirt from stiff paper and dress the lower half of the body.
4 Make the bustle by gluing a pad of cotton wool to the back of the underskirt.
5 Cut the bodice shape from the fabric as shown and dress the upper half of the body.
6 Cut the outer skirt from suitable fabric and stick over the underskirt.
7 Add the cuffs and collar and any other detail in paper or fabric.
8 For a mob cap, cut a circle of material, gather and trim it, and stick it to the hair.
9 Use bits of ribbon, lace and tiny buttons to create various characters and effects.
10 Last of all, fix the head in position.

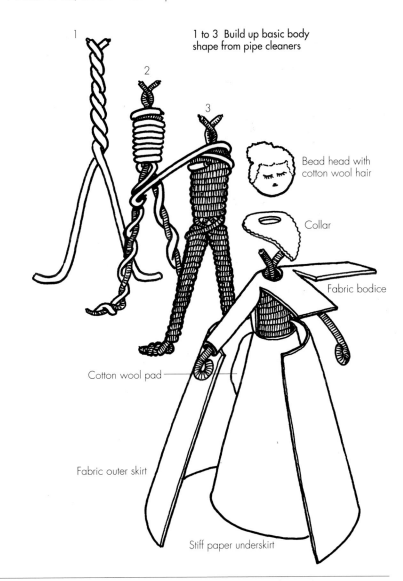

1 to 3 Build up basic body shape from pipe cleaners

Bead head with cotton wool hair

Collar

Fabric bodice

Cotton wool pad

Fabric outer skirt

Stiff paper underskirt

Male

1 Establish the character you want through the hairstyle, whiskers and face.
2 Begin dressing at the feet. Figures are sometimes difficult to stand so make the feet oversized and if they still won't stand, put a blob of Blu-tack under each foot. The boots are made from felt, with card for the soles.
3 Cut two strips of fabric to fit from the ankle to the waist. These will form the trousers. Fold and stick the fabric, with the join inside the leg, one leg at a time.
4 I usually use white paper for the dicky and the collar.
5 Cut the jacket and trousers from fabric.
6 Use black paper for the lapels.
7 Attach the head.

Stage dolls

For these, the male and female dolls follow the same basic pattern.

Parasols
I stiffened circles of fabric in a mixture of PVA glue and water, and then dried them in egg rings to mould them into a curve. For the handles, pierce the centre of each circle with a cocktail stick, and top each stick with a small bead. Draw the spokes on with pen or pencil.

Method

1 From the card, cut out each side of the doll separately. This allows you to have the arms and legs in different positions.

2 Glue the two halves together, with slivers of balsa between them. For female dolls, this balsa should be narrow at thehead and should widen as it goes to the base. For male dolls, it should be narrow at the head and widen until it reaches the legs. Each leg should then be backed with a separate piece of balsa.

3 Hat brims are made from circles of card with a central hole cut out. Glue the hat brim in place.

4 Mix some Polyfilla to a cream consistency and paint it on and around the hat brim to round it out.

5 Paint the Polyfilla onto the face and body to build up character and expression.

6 When the figures are dry, paint on their hair, facial features and clothes, and add the odd touch of lace trimmings and feathers, especially to the ladies' hats.

7 Apply a coat of matt varnish for protection, just in case they get wet.

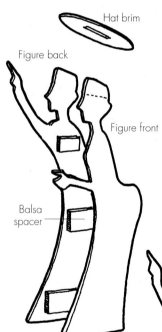

Hat brim

Figure back

Figure front

Balsa spacer

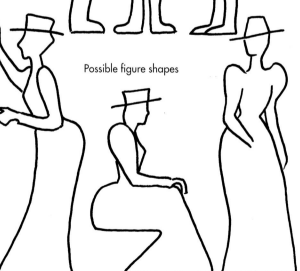

Possible figure shapes

Materials
Card, light
Balsa
Polyfilla
Paint
Lace trimmings
Feathers
Varnish

Henryetta's boots

One of Henryetta's nastier habits is to kick off her boots when she relaxes. These boots are not so dissimilar to the Doc Martens that are popular today, so if you are having trouble getting them to look right, you could model them on these.

Materials
Writing paper
Cotton
Card, firm
Fimo or Plasticine

Method

1 Cut two lengths of paper to the height you want your boots, and just long enough to wrap around a pencil and have the ends meet.
2 Making one boot at a time, wrap the paper around a pencil and lace it up with a needle and cotton. Leave spare cotton at the top to tie the laces. Now you have the leg of the boot.
3 Make the second boot leg.
4 While the legs are still around the pencil, stand them on the card, trace their outline and cut soles to fit, extending them in front for the foot and toe piece.
5 Cut heels from the card and glue these in place.
6 Mould a shoe shape from the Fimo or Plasticine and glue this to the sole.
7 With the pencil still in place, force the leg into the back of the moulded shoe.
8 Lift the pencil a little, then push it down hard to give the boot a wrinkled look.
9 Glue the leg into place.
10 Cut a tongue from the paper and glue this into place.
11 Spray or hand paint.

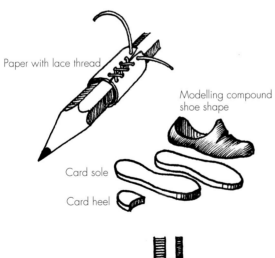

Paper with lace thread

Modelling compound shoe shape

Card sole

Card heel

Paper fitted and rumpled before removing pencil

20 Making Plants and Pots

P lants were an essential part of the Victorian household. Ferns, palms and aspidistra were the most popular, though this had more to do with their hardiness than with their appearance – the fumes from Victorian heaters and lamps were not conducive to a plant's survival.

Don't restrict your plants to being house plants. Create your own garden, fill a conservatory, or make a window box! Plants will always give a sense of life, however they are used.

Plants

There are many ways and many materials you can use to produce mini plants. Here are just a few of them!

Gutta percha

Wire

Cut to shape

Scent bottle top

Alternatives

1 Use gutta percha. This is a roll of green tape, similar to green Sellotape or Scotch tape, available from florists. It is normally used for binding stalks, but works well cut into scale leaves and stuck either side of fine wire. You can build up individual stems into a pot plant.

2 What about recycling? Instead of throwing your used tea leaves out, dry them. If you dip twigs or grape stalks into glue and then into your tea leaves you will have lovely plants.

3 Garden centres sell tiny dried flowers which can be very effective.

4 Lichens sold in model railway shops are excellent, keep their colour and can be used either en masse or teased out to make garlands.

5 Aquarium suppliers have some wonderful mini plants for fish tanks, both plastic and dried.

6 Remembering my early attempts to cook in a microwave, when some dehydrated broccoli floated toward the ceiling, I experimented with microwaving useful looking twigs and sprigs. I found success! They stay firm and keep their colour. Place them in the microwave with a separate container of water and cook them on a low setting for two sessions of four minutes. Remove and spray with hair lacquer.

7 Keep any green plastic bags. These can be rolled and cut to give ferns and fronds.

Pots

Being a potter, I made some of my own pots by throwing the solid shapes on the wheel and then slip casting and biscuit firing them, but if you're not interested in that, here are some alternative ideas for obtaining pots. Whichever pots you use, secure your plants with Plasticine, and cover the Plasticine with earth.

Alternatives

1 There are some excellent scale flowerpots on the market, and you can find tiny ceramic or plastic pots in charity shops.
2 Upended bottle tops make good pots.
3 Small candlesticks turned upside down make lovely raised flower containers.
4 Add chains to single portion cream pots for wonderful hanging baskets.
5 Small knob drawer handles, upended, also make good pots. If they tend to roll, secure them with Blu-Tack.

Piece of green plastic bag, rolled

Small drawer handle

Metric Conversion Table

Inches to Millimetres and Centimetres

MM – millimetres   CM – centimetres

Inches	MM	CM	Inches	CM	Inches	CM
⅛	3	0.3	9	22.9	30	76.2
¼	6	0.6	10	25.4	31	78.7
⅜	10	1.0	11	27.9	32	81.3
½	13	1.3	12	30.5	33	83.8
⅝	16	1.6	13	33.0	34	86.4
¾	19	1.9	14	35.6	35	88.9
⅞	22	2.2	15	38.1	36	91.4
1	25	2.5	16	40.6	37	94.0
1¼	32	3.2	17	43.2	38	96.5
1½	38	3.8	18	45.7	39	99.1
1¾	44	4.4	19	48.3	40	101.6
2	51	5.1	20	50.8	41	104.1
2½	64	6.4	21	53.3	42	106.7
3	76	7.6	22	55.9	43	109.2
3½	89	8.9	23	58.4	44	111.8
4	102	10.2	24	61.0	45	114.3
4½	114	11.4	25	63.5	46	116.8
5	127	12.7	26	66.0	47	119.4
6	152	15.2	27	68.6	48	121.9
7	178	17.8	28	71.1	49	124.5
8	203	20.3	29	73.7	50	127.0

About the Author

Since completing her studies at art school, Patricia King has continued leading her eventful life in the art and craft world. She has worked as a display artist and window dresser, in an advertising art studio and as a teacher. On returning to the UK after living in the USA for three years, she taught pottery and crafts to nursery nurses at two colleges of further education.

Married with three children and an increasing number of grandchildren, she contributes a regular miniatures column to a craft magazine, writes and illustrates stories, and has made a video on making miniatures from odds and ends.

Amongst other things, she arranges displays for pottery and crafts exhibitions, and paints backgrounds for local amateur dramatic societies. She exhibits at craft fairs to show people how to create things rather than to sell, as her advice is always, 'Don't buy it, you can make it!'

Her first book, *Creating A Miniature World*, was republished in a revised and expanded form under the title *Making Dolls' House Furniture*.

Titles available from Guild of Master Craftsman Publications Ltd

Books

Woodworking Plans and Projects
  Guild of Master Craftsman Publications
40 More Woodworking Plans and Projects
  Guild of Master Craftsman Publications
Woodworking Crafts Annual
  Guild of Master Craftsman Publications
Woodworkers' Career and Educational Source Book
  Guild of Master Craftsman Publications
Woodworkers' Courses & Source Book
  Guild of Master Craftsman Publications
Woodturning Techniques Guild of Master Craftsman Publications
Useful Woodturning Projects
  Guild of Master Craftsman Publications
Green Woodwork Mike Abbott
Easy to Make Dolls' House Accessories Andrea Barham
Making Little Boxes from Wood John Bennett
Furniture Restoration and Repair for Beginners Kevin Jan Bonner
Woodturning Jewellery Hilary Bowen
The Incredible Router Jeremy Broun
Electric Woodwork Jeremy Broun
Woodcarving: A Complete Course Ron Buttefield
Making Fine Furniture: Projects Tom Darby
Restoring Rocking Horses Clive Green & Anthony Drew
Heraldic Miniature Knights Peter Greenhill
Make Your Own Dolls' House Furniture Maurice Harper
Practical Crafts: Seat Weaving Ricky Holdstock
Multi-centre Woodturning Ray Hopper
Complete Woodfinishing Ian Hosker
Woodturning: A Source Book of Shapes John Hunnex

Making Shaker Furniture Barry Jackson
Upholstery: A Complete Course David James
Upholstery Techniques and Projects David James
The Upholsterer's Pocket Reference Book David James
Designing and Making Wooden Toys Terry Kelly
Making Dolls' House Furniture Patricia King
Making and Modifying Woodworking Tools Jim Kingshott
The Workshop Jim Kingshott
Sharpening: The Complete Guide Jim Kingshott
Turning Wooden Toys Terry Lawrence
Making Board, Peg and Dice Games Jeff & Jennie Loader
Making Wooden Toys and Games Jeff & Jennie Loader
The Complete Dolls' House Book Jean Nisbett
The Secrets of the Dolls' House Makers Jean Nisbett
Wildfowl Carving, Volume 1 Jim Pearce
Make Money from Woodturning Ann & Bob Phillips
Guide to Marketing Jack Pigden
Woodcarving Tools, Materials and Equipment Chris Pye
Making Tudor Dolls' Houses Derek Rowbottom
Making Georgian Dolls' Houses Derek Rowbottom
Making Period Dolls' House Furniture Derek & Sheila Rowbottom
Woodturning: A Foundation Course Keith Rowley
Turning Miniatures in Wood John Sainsbury
Pleasure and Profit from Woodturning Reg Sherwin
Making Unusual Miniatures Graham Spalding
Woodturning Wizardry David Springett
Adventures in Woodturning David Springett
Furniture Projects Rod Wales
Decorative Woodcarving Jeremy Williams

Videos

Dennis White Teaches Woodturning
Part 1 Turning Between Centres
Part 2 Turning Bowls
Part 3 Boxes, Goblets and Screw Threads
Part 4 Novelties and Projects
Part 5 Classic Profiles
Part 6 Twists and Advanced Turning
John Jordan Bowl Turning

John Jordan   Hollow Turning
Jim Kingshott   Sharpening the Professional Way
Jim Kingshott   Sharpening Turning and Carving Tools
Ray Gonzalez   Carving a Figure: The Female Form
David James   The Traditional Upholstery Workshop
                   Part I: Drop-in and Pinstuffed Seats
David James   The Traditional Upholstery Workshop
                   Part II: Stuffover Upholstery

Guild of Master Craftsman Publications regularly produces new books on a wide range of woodworking and craft subjects,
and an increasing number of specialist magazines, all available on subscription:

Magazines

WOODTURNING   WOODCARVING   BUSINESSMATTERS

All these publications are available through bookshops and newsagents,
or may be ordered by post from the publishers at
166 High Street, Lewes, East Sussex BN7 1XU,
Telephone (01273) 477374, Fax (01273) 478606
Credit card orders are accepted.

PLEASE WRITE OR PHONE FOR A FREE CATALOGUE